Whatever mitigates the woes or increases the happiness of others, this is my criterion of goodness; and whatever injures society at large, or any individual in it, this is my measure of iniquity.

Burns.

ROBERT BURNS
1759-1796

Songs from
ROBERT BURNS

1759-1796

A Selection, with a
Foreword by
G. F. MAINE

COLLINS
LONDON AND GLASGOW

Published by Collins
An imprint of HarperCollins Publishers
Westerhill Road
Bishopbriggs
Glasgow G64 2QT
www.harpercollins.co.uk
collins.reference@harpercollins.co.uk

2nd edition 2016
© Collins 1947

Originally published in 1947 as Songs from Robert Burns

Collins® is a registered trademark of HarperCollins Publishers Ltd

A catalogue record for this book is available from the British Library

ISBN 978-0-00-821058-8

10 9 8 7 6 5 4 3 2 1

Printed in China at R R Donnelley APS Co. Ltd

MIX
Paper from
responsible sources
FSC™ C007454

FSC™ is a non-profit international organisation established to promote the
responsible management of the world's forests. Products carrying the FSC
label are independently certified to assure consumers that they come from
forests that are managed to meet the social, economic and ecological needs
of present and future generations, and other controlled sources.

Find out more about HarperCollins and the environment at
www.harpercollins.co.uk/green

FOREWORD

BURNS wrote his first love song, " Handsome Nell," to Nellie Kirkpatrick with whom he worked at the harvest as a boy of fourteen. It is not to be compared for depth of passion and beauty of feeling with the love verses on Clarinda, which are among the most moving in the language, but Burns looked back upon it fondly as to his first love. For him that springtime of youth, when the soul still slumbered and the hounds of passion were as yet unleashed, was a dream of poetry and innocence.

He had pictured himself when young " as spending his manhood in labour, love-making, and poetry, and his old age as a sort of Edie Ochiltree." But life, which should have been full, adventurous, rewarding, made sport of his dreams, and in the three-act drama of Ayrshire where he was born, Edinburgh where he was fêted, and Dumfries where he died, we see him goaded along upon a road that was pleasant enough in places, pleasant because of good company, enlivening conversation and fair women, but, for one of his temperament, a road that was full of pitfalls. His vigorous spirit was ranged against an environment which he found too narrow and circumscribing, too orderly and

orthodox, too overburdened by its inheritance
from the past. In the words of Stevenson, " he
had no genteel timidities in the conduct of his
life."

Did the period of his sojourn in Edinburgh,
his philanderings with Clarinda and his travel-
ling in the highlands with Willie Nichol bring
irremediable hurt to his muse ? Some would
answer yes categorically. His habits of industry
gave place to habits of pleasure, and his own
opinion was that his mind was " enervated to
an alarming degree by idleness and dissipa-
tion."

Yet the paradox of how to reconcile the
genius of Burns with the character of Burns
need cause us no disquiet, for the genius in
which we delight is independent of character,
and we must learn to condone in the person-
ality weaknesses which seem in painful dis-
cordance with the idealism of the indwelling
spirit. So it was with Byron and Shelley and
a hundred others. The imaginative tempera-
ment brought face to face with actualities is
too frequently caught and fettered by the vices
of the world, but genius has a permanence and
universality which disarms criticism.

Burns himself would have been the first to
agree with the verdict that he acted like a fool
while he wrote like an angel—and not always
like an angel—that he covered his sensitivity
with arrogance, and that his indiscretions were
as much deliberate assertions of his indepen-

dence, as they were natural impulses. All too clearly, as the wheel of life turned inexorably, he perceived that paradise is attained only by way of the chastening fire of purgatory, and there is no more heartrending picture than that of Burns as he appeared in the third act of the drama, conscious of his failing powers, yet helpless to recapture the fire and spirit of his muse. Towards the end he became more scrupulous as an artist, and some two months before his death he asked Thomson to send back all his manuscripts for revisal, saying that he would rather write five songs to his taste than twice that number otherwise.

There have been many evaluations of the work of the poet and there will be many more, but none will gainsay that his heart was attuned to melody and that in prompting him to hold fast to the tradition of Scots music, his native good sense saved him from the false elegance of his day. In the best of the lyrics we have the flower and perfection of his art. They, more than all else, have won for him an abiding place in the hearts of the Scottish people. They are eloquent of the soul from which they sprung—instinct with passion, with tenderness and with that human gift of understanding which is synonymous with true greatness. It is the humanity of Burns, his greatheartedness, his proud independence, his strong democratic feeling, and his abiding faith in God, that endear him to his countrymen.

7

He wrote prose as well as poetry, but how-
ever much we may admire its technical excel-
lence, it does not ring true, and the same may
be said of his poems in English. It is far other-
wise with the poems and songs in the dialect of
his own country, for be the subject ever so
trivial, it is touched with promethean fire and
becomes immortal. The poetry which we find
most satisfying is that which contains the fullest
reaction to life, and Burns found inspiration in
his own environment.

The poet's response to beauty is readier and
more intense than that of less gifted humanity,
and in the heritage which he has left us we
are able to share vicariously in his heightened
awareness and become more fully alive.

G. F. MAINE.

CONTENTS

CONTENTS

CONTENTS

CONTENTS

MARY MORISON

O Mary, at thy window be,
  It is the wish'd, the trysted hour!
Those smiles and glances let me see,
  That make the miser's treasure poor:
How blythely wad I bide the stoure,
  A weary slave frae sun to sun,
Could I the rich reward secure,
  The lovely Mary Morison.

Yestreen, when to the trembling string
  The dance gaed thro' the lighted ha',
To thee my fancy took its wing,
  I sat, but neither heard nor saw:
Tho' this was fair, and that was braw,
  And yon the toast of a' the town,
I sigh'd, and said among them a',
  ' Ye are na Mary Morison.'

Oh, Mary, canst thou wreck his peace,
  Wha for thy sake wad gladly die?
Or canst thou break that heart of his,
  Whase only faut is loving thee?
If love for love thou wilt na gie,
  At least be pity to me shown;
A thought ungentle canna be
  The thought o' Mary Morison.

MY LUVE IS LIKE A RED, RED ROSE

My Luve is like a red, red rose,
   That's newly sprung in June :
My Luve is like the melodie,
   That's sweetly play'd in tune.

As fair art thou, my bonnie lass,
   So deep in luve am I ;
And I will luve thee still, my Dear,
   Till a' the seas gang dry.

Till a' the seas gang dry, my Dear,
   And the rocks melt wi' the sun ;
And I will luve thee still, my Dear,
   While the sands o' life shall run.

And fare-thee-weel, my only Luve !
   And fare-thee-weel, a while !
And I will come again, my Luve,
   Tho' 'twere ten thousand mile !

AFTON WATER

Flow gently, sweet Afton ! among thy green
    braes,
Flow gently, I'll sing thee a song in thy praise ;
My Mary's asleep by thy murmuring stream,
Flow gently, sweet Afton, disturb not her dream.

Thou stock-dove whose echo resounds thro' the
    glen,
Ye wild whistling blackbirds, in yon thorny
    den,
Thou green-crested lapwing thy screaming
    forbear,
I charge you, disturb not my slumbering Fair.

How lofty, sweet Afton, thy neighbouring hills,
Far mark'd with the courses of clear, winding
    rills ;
There daily I wander as noon rises high,
My flocks and my Mary's sweet cot in my eye.

How pleasant thy banks and green valleys
    below,
Where, wild in the woodlands, the primroses
    blow ;
There oft, as mild Ev'ning weeps over the lea,
The sweet-scented birk shades my Mary and
    me.

Thy crystal stream, Afton, how lovely it glides,
And winds by the cot where my Mary resides ;
How wanton thy waters her snowy feet lave,
As, gathering sweet flowerets, she stems thy
    clear wave.

Flow gently, sweet Afton, among thy green
    braes,
Flow gently, sweet river, the theme of my lays ;
My Mary's asleep by thy murmuring stream,
Flow gently, sweet Afton, disturb not her
    dream.

THE SILVER TASSIE

Go, fetch to me a pint o' wine,
   And fill it in a silver tassie ;
That I may drink before I go,
   A service to my bonnie lassie.
The boat rocks at the pier o' Leith ;
   Fu' loud the wind blaws frae the Ferry ;
The ship rides by the Berwick-law,
   And I maun leave my bonnie Mary.

The trumpets sound, the banners fly,
   The glittering spears are rankèd ready :
The shouts o' war are heard afar,
   The battle closes deep and bloody ;
It's not the roar o' sea or shore,
   Wad mak me langer wish to tarry ;
Nor shouts o' war that's heard afar—
   It's leaving thee, my bonnie Mary !

HIGHLAND MARY

Ye banks and braes and streams around
   The castle o' Montgomery !
Green be your woods, and fair your flowers,
   Your waters never drumlie :
There Simmer first unfauld her robes,
   And there the langest tarry ;
For there I took the last Fareweel
   O' my sweet Highland Mary.

How sweetly bloom'd the gay, green birk,
   How rich the hawthorn's blossom,
As underneath their fragrant shade,
   I clasp'd her to my bosom !
The golden Hours on angel wings,
   Flew o'er me and my Dearie ;
For dear to me, as light and life,
   Was my sweet Highland Mary.

Wi' mony a vow, and lock'd embrace,
   Our parting was fu' tender ;
And, pledging aft to meet again,
   We tore oursels asunder ;
But oh ! fell Death's untimely frost,
   That nipt my Flower sae early !
Now green's the sod, and cauld's the clay
   That wraps my Highland Mary.

O pale, pale now, those rosy lips,
    I aft hae kiss'd sae fondly !
And clos'd for ay, the sparkling glance
    That dwelt on me sae kindly !
And mouldering now in silent dust,
    That heart that lo'ed me dearly !
But still within my bosom's core
    Shall live my Highland Mary.

TO MARY IN HEAVEN

THOU ling'ring star, with less'ning ray,
    That lov'st to greet the early morn,
Again thou usher'st in the day
    My Mary from my soul was torn.
O Mary ! dear departed shade !
    Where is thy place of blissful rest ?
See'st thou thy lover lowly laid ?
    Hear'st thou the groans that rend his
        breast ?

That sacred hour can I forget ?
    Can I forget the hallow'd grove,
Where, by the winding Ayr, we met,
    To live one day of parting love ?
Eternity can not efface
    Those records dear of transports past,
Thy image at our last embrace,
    Ah ! little thought we 'twas our last !

Ayr, gurgling, kiss'd his pebbled shore,
  O'erhung with wild-woods, thickening green;
The fragrant birch and hawthorn hoar,
  'Twin'd amorous round the raptur'd scene :
The flowers sprang wanton to be prest,
  The birds sang love on every spray ;
Till too, too soon, the glowing west,
  Proclaim'd the speed of wingèd day.

Still o'er these scenes my mem'ry wakes,
  And fondly broods with miser-care ;
Time but th' impression stronger makes,
  As streams their channels deeper wear.
My Mary ! dear departed shade !
  Where is thy place of blissful rest ?
See'st thou thy lover lowly laid ?
  Hear'st thou the groans that rend his breast ?

AE FOND KISS

(Parting Song to Clarinda)

Ae fond kiss, and then we sever ;
Ae fareweel, and then for ever !
Deep in heart-wrung tears I'll pledge thee !
Warring sighs and groans I'll wage thee !
Who shall say that Fortune grieves him,
While the star of hope she leaves him ?
Me, nae cheerful twinkle lights me ;
Dark despair around benights me.

I'll ne'er blame my partial fancy,
Naething could resist my Nancy :
But to see her was to love her ;
Love but her, and love for ever.
Had we ne'er lov'd sae kindly,
Had we never lov'd sae blindly,
Never met—or never parted,
We had ne'er been broken-hearted.

Fare-thee-weel, thou first and fairest !
Fare-thee-weel, thou best and dearest !
Thine be ilka joy and treasure,
Peace, Enjoyment, Love, and Pleasure !
Ae fond kiss, and then we sever !
Ae fareweel, alas, for ever !
Deep in heart-wrung tears I'll pledge thee,
Warring sighs and groans I'll wage thee.

MY NANIE'S AWA'

Now in her green mantle blythe Nature
    arrays,
And listens the lambkins that bleat o'er the
    braes,
While birds warble welcome in ilka green shaw,
But to me it's delightless—my Nanie's awa'.

The snawdrap and primrose our woodlands
    adorn,
And violets bathe in the weet o' the morn ;
They pain my sad bosom, sae sweetly they
    blaw,
They mind me o' Nanie—and Nanie's awa'.

Thou lav'rock that springs frae the dews of the
    lawn
The shepherd to warn o' the gray-breaking
    dawn,
And thou mellow mavis that hails the night-fa',
Give over for pity—my Nanie's awa'.

Come Autumn, sae pensive, in yellow and gray,
And soothe me wi' tidings o' Nature's decay :
The dark, dreary Winter, and wild-driving
    snaw
Alane can delight me—now Nanie's awa'.

THE BANKS O' DOON

Ye banks and braes o' bonnie Doon,
　How can ye bloom sae fresh and fair ?
How can ye chant, ye little birds,
　And I sae weary fu' o' care ?
Thou'll break my heart, thou warbling bird,
　That wantons thro' the flowering thorn :
Thou minds me o' departed joys,
　Departed never to return.

Aft hae I rov'd by bonnie Doon,
　To see the rose and woodbine twine ;
And ilka bird sang o' its Luve,
　And fondly sae did I o' mine ;
Wi' lightsome heart I pu'd a rose
　Fu' sweet upon its thorny tree !
And my fause Luver staw my rose,
　But ah ! he left the thorn wi' me.

OF A' THE AIRTS

Of a' the airts the wind can blaw,
  I dearly like the west,
For there the bonnie lassie lives,
  The lassie I lo'e best :
There's wild-woods grow, and rivers row,
  And mony a hill between :
But day and night my fancy's flight
  Is ever wi' my Jean.

I see her in the dewy flowers,
  I see her sweet and fair :
I hear her in the tunefu' birds,
  I hear her charm the air :
There's not a bonnie flower that springs,
  By fountain, shaw, or green ;
There's not a bonnie bird that sings
  But minds me o' my Jean.

RANTIN', ROVIN' ROBIN

THERE was a lad was born in Kyle,
But whatna day o' whatna style,
I doubt it's hardly worth the while
    To be sae nice wi' Robin.
        Robin was, etc.

Chorus

Robin was a rovin' boy,
    Rantin', rovin', rantin', rovin',
Robin was a rovin' boy,
    Rantin', rovin', Robin !

Our monarch's hindmost year but ane
Was five-and-twenty days begun,
'Twas then a blast o' Janwar' win'
    Blew hansel in on Robin.
        Robin was, etc.

The gossip keekit in his loof,
Quo' scho, ' Wha lives will see the proof,
This waly boy will be nae coof :
    I think we'll ca' him Robin.'
        Robin was, etc.

' He'll hae misfortunes great an' sma',
But ay a heart aboon them a'.
He'll be a credit till us a'—
    We'll a' be proud o' Robin.'
        Robin was, etc.

' But sure as three times three mak nine,
I see by ilka score and line,
This chap will dearly like our kin',
    So leeze me on thee ! Robin.'
        Robin was, etc.

GREEN GROW THE RASHES

Chorus

Green grow the rashes, O ;
    Green grow the rashes, O ;
The sweetest hours that e'er I spend,
    Are spent among the lasses, O.

THERE's naught but care on ev'ry han',
    In every hour that passes, O :
What signifies the life o' man,
    An' 'twere na for the lasses, O :
        Green grow, etc.

The warl'y race may riches chase,
    An' riches still may fly them, O ;
An' tho' at last they catch them fast,
    Their hearts can ne'er enjoy them, O.
        Green grow, etc.

But gie me a cannie hour at e'en,
    My arms about my dearie, O ;
An' warl'y cares, an' warl'y men,
    May a' gae tapsalteerie, O !
        Green grow, etc.

27

For you sae douce, ye sneer at this,
 Ye're naught but senseless asses, O :
The wisest man the warl' e'er saw,
 He dearly lov'd the lasses, O.
        Green grow, etc.

Auld Nature swears, the lovely dears
 Her noblest work she classes, O,
Her prentice han' she try'd on man,
 An' then she made the lasses, O.
        Green grow, etc.

A MAN'S A MAN FOR A' THAT

Is there for honest Poverty
  That hings his head, an' a' that ;
The coward slave—we pass him by,
  We dare be poor for a' that !
For a' that, an' a' that,
  Our toils obscure an' a' that,
The rank is but the guinea's stamp,
  The Man's the gowd for a' that.

What though on hamely fare we dine,
  Wear hodden gray, an' a' that ;
Gie fools their silks, and knaves their wine,
  A Man's a Man for a' that :
For a' that, an' a' that,
  Their tinsel show, an' a' that ;
The honest man, tho' e'er sae poor,
  Is king o' men for a' that.

Ye see yon birkie ca'd 'a lord,'
  Wha struts, an' stares, an' a' that ;
Tho' hundreds worship at his word,
  He's but a coof for a' that :
For a' that, an' a' that,
  His ribband, star, an' a' that ;
The man o' independent mind
  He looks an' laughs at a' that.

A prince can mak a belted knight,
    A marquis, duke, an' a' that ;
But an honest man's aboon his might,
    Gude faith, he mauna fa' that !
For a' that, an' a' that,
    Their dignities, an' a' that ;
The pith o' sense, an' pride o' worth,
    Are higher rank than a' that.

Then let us pray that come it may
    (As come it will for a' that),
That Sense and Worth o'er a' the earth,
    Shall bear the gree, an' a' that.
For a' that, an' a' that,
    It's comin' yet for a' that,
That Man to Man, the world o'er,
    Shall brothers be for a' that.

SCOTS WHA HAE

(Robert Bruce's March to Bannockburn)

Scots, wha hae wi' WALLACE bled,
Scots, wham Bruce has aften led,
Welcome to your gory bed,
    Or to Victorie !
Now's the day and now's the hour ;
See the front o' battle lour ;
See approach proud EDWARD's power—
    Chains and Slaverie !

Wha will be a traitor knave ?
Wha can fill a coward's grave ?
Wha sae base as be a slave ?
    Let him turn and flee !
Wha for Scotland's King and Law,
Freedom's sword will strongly draw,
FREE-MAN stand, or FREE-MAN fa'
    Let him follow me !

By Oppression's woes and pains !
By your Sons in servile chains !
We will drain our dearest veins,
    But they *shall* be free !
Lay the proud Usurpers low !
Tyrants fall in every foe !
LIBERTY's in every blow !
    Let us Do—or Die !

WANDERING WILLIE

Here awa', there awa', wandering Willie,
Here awa', there awa', haud awa' hame ;
Come to my bosom, my ain only dearie,
    Tell me thou bring'st me my Willie the same.
Winter winds blew loud and cauld at our
    parting,
    Fears for my Willie brought tears to my e'e,
Welcome now Simmer, and welcome my Willie,
    The Simmer to Nature, my Willie to me.

Rest, ye wild storms, in the cave of your
    slumbers,
    How your dread howling a lover alarms !
Wauken, ye breezes, row gently, ye billows,
    And waft my dear laddie ance mair to my
    arms.
But oh, if he's faithless, and mind na his Nannie,
    Flow still between us, thou wide roaring
    main !
May I never see it, may I never trow it,
    But, dying, believe that my Willie's my ain.

BRAW LADS O' GALLA WATER

Braw, braw lads on Yarrow braes,
  They rove amang the blooming heather ;
But Yarrow braes, nor Ettrick shaws
  Can match the lads o' Galla Water.

But there is ane, a secret ane,
  Aboon them a' I lo'e him better :
And I'll be his, and he'll be mine,
  The bonnie lad o' Galla Water.

Altho' his daddie was nae laird,
  And tho' I hae na meikle tocher,
Yet rich in kindest, truest love,
  We'll tent our flocks by Galla Water.

It ne'er was wealth, it ne'er was wealth,
  That coft contentment, peace, or pleasure ;
The bands and bliss o' mutual love,
  O that's the chiefest warld's treasure.

B

CA' THE YOWES TO THE KNOWES

Chorus

Ca' the yowes to the knowes,
Ca' them where the heather grows,
Ca' them where the burnie rowes,
   My bonnie Dearie.

HARK, the mavis' e'ening sang,
Sounding Clouden's woods amang;
Then a-faulding let us gang,
   My bonnie Dearie.
         Ca' the yowes, etc.

We'll gae down by Clouden side,
Thro' the hazels spreading wide,
O'er the waves that sweetly glide,
   To the moon sae clearly.
         Ca' the yowes, etc.

Yonder Clouden's silent towers,
Where, **at moonshine's midnight hours,**
O'er the dewy bending flowers,
   Fairies dance sae cheery.
         Ca' the yowes, etc.

Ghaist nor bogle shalt thou fear,
Thou'rt to Love and Heav'n sae dear
Nocht of ill may come thee near ;
  My bonnie Dearie.
            Ca' the yowes, etc.

Fair and lovely as thou art,
Thou hast stown my very heart ;
I can die—but canna part
  My bonnie Dearie.
            Ca' the yowes, etc.

JOHN ANDERSON, MY JO

JOHN ANDERSON, my jo, John,
  When we were first acquent ;
Your locks were like the raven,
  Your bonnie brow was brent ;
But now your brow is beld, John,
  Your locks are like the snaw ;
But blessings on your frosty pow,
  John Anderson, my jo.

John Anderson, my jo, John,
  We clamb the hill thegither ;
And mony a cantie day, John,
  We've had wi' ane anither :
Now we maun totter down, John,
  And hand in hand we'll go,
And sleep thegither at the foot,
  John Anderson, my jo.

THE BIRKS OF ABERFELDY

Chorus
Bonnie lassie, will ye go,
Will ye go, will ye go,
Bonnie lassie, will ye go,
  To the birks of Aberfeldy !

Now Simmer blinks on flowery braes,
And o'er the crystal streamlet plays ;
Come, let us spend the lightsome days,
  In the birks of Aberfeldy.
            Bonnie lassie, etc.

The little birdies blythely sing,
While o'er their heads the hazels hing,
Or lightly flit on wanton wing,
  In the birks of Aberfeldy.
            Bonnie lassie, etc.

The braes ascend like lofty wa's,
The foamy stream deep-roaring fa's,
O'erhung wi' fragrant spreading shaws—
  The birks of Aberfeldy.
            Bonnie lassie, etc.

The hoary cliffs are crown'd wi' flowers,
White o'er the linns the burnie pours,
And rising, weets wi' misty showers
   The birks of Aberfeldy.
          Bonnie lassie, etc.

Let Fortune's gifts at random flee,
They ne'er shall draw a wish frae me ;
Supremely blest wi' love and thee,
   In the birks of Aberfeldy.
          Bonnie lassie, etc.

O WERT THOU IN THE CAULD BLAST

O WERT thou in the cauld blast,
  On yonder lea, on yonder lea,
My plaidie to the angry airt,
  I'd shelter thee, I'd shelter thee ;
Or did Misfortune's bitter storms
  Around thee blaw, around thee blaw,
Thy bield should be my bosom,
  To share it a', to share it a'.

Or were I in the wildest waste,
  Sae black and bare, sae black and bare,
The desert were a Paradise,
  If thou wert there, if thou wert there ;
Or were I Monarch o' the globe,
  Wi' thee to reign, wi' thee to reign,
The brightest jewel in my crown
  Wad be my Queen, wad be my Queen.

UP IN THE MORNING EARLY

CAULD blaws the wind frae east to west,
   The drift is driving sairly ;
Sae loud and shill 's I hear the blast—
   I'm sure it's winter fairly.

Chorus

Up in the morning's no for me,
   Up in the morning early ;
When a' the hills are cover'd wi' snaw,
   I'm sure it's winter fairly.

The birds sit chittering in the thorn,
   A' day they fare but sparely ;
And lang's the night frae e'en to morn—
   I'm sure it's winter fairly.
         Up in the morning's, etc.

FAREWELL TO THE HIGHLANDS

Farewell to the Highlands, farewell to the
   north,
The birthplace of Valour, the country of
   Worth ;
Wherever I wander, wherever I rove,
The hills of the Highlands for ever I love.
   My heart's in the Highlands, etc.

Chorus

My heart's in the Highlands, my heart is not
   here,
My heart's in the Highlands, a-chasing the
   deer ;
A-chasing the wild deer, and following the roe,
My heart's in the Highlands wherever I go.

Farewell to the mountains, high-cover'd with
   snow,
Farewell to the straths and green valleys below ;
Farewell to the forests and wild-hanging woods,
Farewell to the torrents and loud-pouring
   floods.
   My heart's in the Highlands, etc.

DUNCAN GRAY

Duncan Gray cam here to woo,
   Ha, ha, the wooing o't,
On blythe Yule-night when we were fou,
   Ha, ha, the wooing o't,
Maggie coost her head fu' high,
Look'd asklent and unco skeigh
Gart poor Duncan stand abeigh ;
   Ha, ha, the wooing o't.

Duncan fleech'd and Duncan pray'd ;
   Ha, ha, the wooing o't,
Meg was deaf as Ailsa Craig,
   Ha, ha, the wooing o't :
Duncan sigh'd baith out and in,
Grat his e'en baith blear't and blin',
Spak o' lowpin' o'er a linn ;
   Ha, ha, the wooing o't.

Time and Chance are but a tide,
   Ha, ha, the wooing o't,
Slighted love is sair to bide,
   Ha, ha, the wooing o't :
Shall I like a fool, quoth he,
For a haughty hizzie die ?
She may gae to—France for me !
   Ha, ha, the wooing o't.

How it comes let doctors tell,
  Ha, ha, the wooing o't ;
Meg grew sick, as he grew hale,
  Ha, ha, the wooing o't.
Something in her bosom wrings,
For relief a sigh she brings :
And oh ! her een they spak sic things .
  Ha, ha, the wooing o't.

Duncan was a lad o' grace,
  Ha, ha, the wooing o't ;
Maggie's was a piteous case,
  Ha, ha, the wooing o't ;
Duncan could na be her death,
Swelling Pity smoor'd his wrath ;
Now they're crouse and canty baith,
  Ha, ha, the wooing o't.

POORTITH CAULD, AND RESTLESS LOVE

O POORTITH cauld, and restless love,
 Ye wrack my peace between ye ;
Yet poortith a' I could forgive,
 An' 'twere na for my Jeanie.

Chorus

O why should Fate sic pleasure have,
 Life's dearest bands untwining ?
Or why sae sweet a flower as love
 Depend on Fortune's shining ?

The warld's wealth, when I think on,
 Its pride and a' the lave o't ;
O fie on silly coward man,
 That he should be the slave o't !
  O why, etc.

Her een, sae bonnie blue, betray
 How she repays my passion ;
But prudence is her o'erword ay,
 She talks o' rank and fashion.
  O why, etc.

O wha can prudence think upon,
  And sic a lassie by him ?
O wha can prudence think upon
  And sae in love as I am ?
      O why, etc.

How blest the simple cotter's fate !
  He woo's his artless dearie ;
The silly bogles, wealth and state,
  Can never make him eerie.
      O why, etc.

THE BANKS OF THE DEVON

How pleasant the banks of the clear winding
    Devon,
With green spreading bushes and flow'rs
    blooming fair !
But the boniest flow'r on the banks of the
    Devon
    Was once a sweet bud on the braes of the Ayr.
Mild be the sun on this sweet blushing flower,
    In the gay rosy morn, as it bathes in the dew ;
And gently the fall of the soft vernal shower,
    That steals on the evening each leaf to
    renew !

O spare the dear blossom, ye orient breezes,
    With chill hoary wing as ye usher the dawn ;
And far be thou distant, thou reptile that seizes
    The verdure and pride of the garden or lawn!
Let Bourbon exult in his gay gilded lilies,
    And England triumphant display her proud
    rose :
A fairer than either adorns the green valleys,
    Where Devon, sweet Devon, meandering
    flows.

AULD LANG SYNE

SHOULD auld acquaintance be forgot,
    And never brought to mind ?
Should auld acquaintance be forgot,
    And auld lang syne ?
        For auld, etc.

Chorus
For auld lang syne, my dear,
    For auld lang syne,
We'll tak a cup o' kindness yet,
    For auld lang syne.

And surely ye'll be your pint-stoup !
    And surely I'll be mine !
And we'll tak a cup o' kindness yet,
    For auld lang syne.
        For auld, etc.

We twa hae run about the braes,
    And pou'd the gowans fine ;
But we've wander'd mony a weary fit,
    Sin' auld lang syne.
        For auld, etc.

We twa hae paidl'd in the burn,
    Frae morning sun till dine ;
But seas between us braid hae roar'd
    Sin' auld lang syne.
            For auld, etc.

And there's a hand, my trusty fiere !
    And gies a hand o' thine !
And we'll tak a right gude-willie waught,
    For auld lang syne.
            For auld, etc.

THE GLOOMY NIGHT

THE gloomy night is gathering fast,
Loud roars the wild inconstant blast,
Yon murky cloud is foul with rain,
I see it driving o'er the plain ;
The hunter now has left the moor,
The scatter'd coveys meet secure,
While here I wander, prest with care,
Along the lonely banks of Ayr.

The Autumn mourns her ripening corn
By early Winter's ravage torn ;
Across her placid azure sky,
She sees the scowling tempest fly:
Chill runs my blood to hear it rave,
I think upon the stormy wave,
Where many a danger I must dare,
Far from the bonnie banks of Ayr.

'Tis not the surging billow's roar,
'Tis not that fatal, deadly shore ;
Tho' death in ev'ry shape appear,
The wretched have no more to fear :
But round my heart the ties are bound,
That heart transpierc'd with many a
        wound :
These bleed afresh, those ties I tear,
To leave the bonnie banks of Ayr.

Farewell, old Coila's hills and dales,
Her heathy moors and winding vales ;
The scenes where wretched fancy roves,
Pursuing past unhappy loves !
Farewell, my friends ! Farewell, my foes !
My peace with these, my love with those ;
The bursting tears my heart declare,
Farewell, the bonnie banks of Ayr !

THE FAREWELL

(*The Brethren of St. James's Lodge, Tarbolton*)

Adieu ! a heart-warm fond adieu !
  Dear brothers of the mystic tie !
Ye favour'd, ye enlighten'd few,
  Companions of my social joy !
Tho' I to foreign lands must hie,
  Pursuing Fortune's slidd'ry ba',
With melting heart, and brimful eye,
  I'll mind you still, tho' far awa'.

Oft have I met your social band,
  And spent the cheerful festive night ;
Oft, honour'd with supreme command,
  Presided o'er the sons of light :
And by that hieroglyphic bright,
  Which none but craftsmen ever saw !
Strong memory on my heart shall write
  Those happy scenes when far awa' !

May freedom, harmony, and love
    Unite you in the grand design,
Beneath th' Omniscient eye above,
    The glorious Architect Divine !
That you may keep th' unerring line,
    Still rising by the plummet's law,
Till Order bright completely shine,
    Shall be my pray'r when far awa'.

And You, farewell! whose merits claim,
    Justly, that highest badge to wear !
Heav'n bless your honour'd noble name,
    To Masonry and Scotia dear !
A last request permit me here :
    When yearly ye assemble a',—
One round, I ask it with a tear,
    To him, the Bard that's far awa'.

THE RIGS O' BARLEY

It was upon a Lammas night,
   When corn rigs are bonnie,
Beneath the moon's unclouded light,
   I held awa' to Annie ;
The time flew by, wi' tentless heed ;
   Till, 'tween the late and early,
Wi' sma' persuasion she agreed
   To see me thro' the barley.

Chorus

Corn rigs, an' barley rigs,
   An' corn rigs are bonnie :
I'll ne'er forget that happy night,
   Amang the rigs wi' Annie.

The sky was blue, the wind was still,
   The moon was shining clearly ;
I set her down, wi' right goodwill,
   Amang the rigs o' barley :
I ken't her heart was a' my ain ;
   I lov'd her most sincerely ;
I kiss'd her owre and owre again,
   Amang the rigs o' barley.
      Corn rigs, an' barley rigs, etc.

I lock'd her in my fond embrace ;
   Her heart was beating rarely :
My blessings on that happy place,
   Amang the rigs o' barley !
But by the moon and stars so bright,
   That shone that hour so clearly !
She ay shall bless that happy night
   Amang the rigs o' barley.
       Corn rigs, an' barley rigs, etc.

I hae been blythe wi' comrades dear ;
   I hae been merry drinking ;
I hae been joyfu' gath'rin' gear ;
   I hae been happy thinking :
But a' the pleasures e'er I saw,
   Tho' three times doubl'd fairly—
That happy night was worth them a',
   Amang the rigs o' barley.
       Corn rigs, an' barley rigs, etc.

THE BLUE-EYED LASSIE

I GAED a waefu' gate yestreen,
    A gate I fear I'll dearly rue ;
I gat my death frae twa sweet een,
    Twa lovely een o' bonnie blue.
'Twas not her golden ringlets bright,
    Her lips, like roses wat wi' dew,
Her heaving bosom, lily-white—
    It was her een sae bonnie blue.

She talk'd, she smil'd, my heart she wyl'd;
    She charm'd my soul I wist na how ;
And ay the stound, the deadly wound,
    Cam frae her een sae bonnie blue.
But ' spare to speak, and spare to speed '
    She'll aiblins listen to my vow :
Should she refuse, I'll lay my dead
    To her twa een sae bonnie blue.

O TIBBIE, I HAE SEEN
THE DAY

Chorus

O Tibbie, I hae seen the day,
　Ye wadna been sae shy ;
For laik o' gear ye lightly me,
　But, trowth, I care na by.

YESTREEN I met you on the moor,
　Ye spak na, but gaed by like stoure ;
Ye geck at me because I'm poor,
　But fient a hair care I.
　　　O Tibbie, I hae seen the day, etc.

When comin' hame on Sunday last,
Upon the road as I cam past,
Ye snufft and gae your head a cast—
　But trowth I care't na by.
　　　O Tibbie, I hae seen the day, etc.

I doubt na, lass, but ye may think,
Because ye hae the name o' clink,
That ye can please me at a wink,
　Whene'er ye like to try.
　　　O Tibbie, I hae seen the day, etc.

But sorrow tak him that's sae mean,
Altho' his pouch o' coin were clean,
Wha follows ony saucy quean,
 That looks sae proud and high.
   O Tibbie, I hae seen the day, etc.

Altho' a lad were e'er sae smart,
If that he want the yellow dirt,
Ye'll cast your head anither airt,
 And answer him fu' dry.
   O Tibbie, I hae seen the day, etc.

But if he hae the name o' gear,
Ye'll fasten to him like a brier,
Tho' hardly he, for sense or lear,
 Be better than the kye.
   O Tibbie, I hae seen the day, etc.

But, Tibbie, lass, tak my advice :
Your daddie's gear maks you sae nice ;
The deil a ane wad spier your price,
 Were ye as poor as I.
   O Tibbie, I hae seen the day, etc.

There lives a lass beside yon park,
I'd rather hae her in her sark,
Then you wi' a' your thousand mark ;
 That gars you look sae high.
   O Tibbie, I gae seen the day, etc.

TAM GLEN

My heart is a-breaking, dear Tittie,
  Some counsel unto me come len',
To anger them a' is a pity,
  But what will I do wi' Tam Glen?

I'm thinking, wi' sic a braw fellow,
  In poortith I might mak a fen';
What care I in riches to wallow,
  If I manna marry Tam Glen?

There's Lowrie the Laird o' Dumeller—
  'Gude day to you'—brute! he comes ben:
He brags and he blaws o' his siller,
  But when will he dance like Tam Glen?

My minnie does constantly deave me,
  And bids me beware o' young men;
They flatter, she says, to deceive me,
  But wha can think sae o' Tam Glen?

My daddie says, gin I'll forsake him,
  He'd gie me gude hunder marks ten;
But, if it's ordain'd I maun take him,
  O wha will I get but Tam Glen?

57

Yestreen at the Valentine's dealing,
   My heart to my mou' gied a sten ;
For thrice I drew ane without failing,
   And thrice it was written ' Tam Glen ! '

The last Halloween I was waukin'
   My droukit sark-sleeve, as ye ken,
His likeness came up the house staukin',
   And the very gray breeks o' Tam Glen !

Come, counsel, dear Tittie, don't tarry ;
   I'll gie ye my bonnie black hen,
Gif ye will advise me to marry
   The lad I lo'e dearly, Tam Glen.

CONTENTED WI' LITTLE AND
CANTIE WI' MAIR

CONTENTED wi' little, and cantie wi' mair,
Whene'er I forgather wi' Sorrow and Care,
I gie tham a skelp as they're creepin' alang,
Wi' a cog o' gude swats and an auld Scottish
    sang.

      Chorus.—Contented wi' little, etc.

I whyles claw the elbow o' troublesome
    thought ;
But Man is a soger, and Life is a faught ;
My mirth and gude humour are coin in my
    pouch,
And my Freedom's my Lairdship nae monarch
    dare touch.

      Contented wi' little, etc.

A towmond o' trouble, should that be my fa',
A night o' gude fellowship sowthers it a' :
When at the blythe end o' our journey at last,
Wha the deil ever thinks o' the road he has
    past ?

      Contented wi' little, etc.

Blind chance, let her snapper and stoyte on her
    way ;
Be't to me, be't frae me, e'en let the jade gae :
Come Ease, or come Travail, come Pleasure or
    Pain,
My warst word is : ' Welcome, and welcome
    again ! '

        Contented wi' little, etc.

WHISTLE AND I'LL COME TO YE, MY LAD

Chorus

O whistle an' I'll come to ye, my lad,
O Whistle an' I'll come to ye, my lad,
Tho' faither an' mither an' a' should gae mad,
O whistle an' I'll come to ye, my lad.

BUT warily tent when ye come to court me,
And come nae unless the back-yett be a-jee ;
Syne up the back style, and let naebody see,
And come as ye were na comin' at me,
And come as ye were na comin' to me,
    O whistle an' I'll come, etc.

At kirk, or at market, whene'er ye meet me,
Gang by me as tho' that ye car'd na a flie ;
But steal me a blink o' your bonnie black 'e,
Yet look as ye were na lookin' at me,
Yet look as ye were na lookin' to me,
　　　O whistle an' I'll come, etc.

Ay vow and protest that ye care na for me,
And whyles ye may lightly my beauty a-wee ;
But court na anither tho' jokin' ye be,
For fear that she wyle your fancy frae me,
For fear that she wyle your fancy frae me.
　　　O whistle, an' I'll come, etc.

MEG O' THE MILL

O KEN ye what Meg o' the Mill has gotten,
An' ken ye what Meg o' the Mill has gotten?
She has gotten a coof wi' a claut o' siller,
And broken the heart o' the barley Miller.

The Miller was strappin, the Miller was ruddy;
A heart like a lord, and a hue like a lady;
The Laird was a widdiefu', bleerit knurl;
She's left the guid fellow and ta'en the churl.

The Miller he hecht her a heart leal and loving;
The Laird did address her wi' matter mair
    moving,
A fine pacing horse wi' a clear chained bridle,
A whip by her side, and a bonnie side-saddle.

O wae on the siller, it is sae prevailing;
And wae on the love that is fix'd on a mailen!
A tocher's nae word in a true lover's parle,
But gie me my love, and a fig for the warl!

THE LEA-RIG

WHEN o'er the hill the e'ening star
  Tells bughtin' time is near, my jo,
And owsen frae the furrow'd field
  Return sae dowf and weary O ;
Down by the burn, where birken buds
  Wi' dew are hangin' clear, my jo,
I'll meet thee on the lea-rig,
  My ain kind Dearie O.

At midnight hour, in mirkest glen,
  I'd rove, and ne'er be eerie O,
If thro' that glen I gaed to thee,
  My ain kind Dearie O ;
Altho' the night were ne'er sae wild,
  And I were ne'er sae weary O,
I'll meet thee on the lea-rig,
  My ain kind Dearie O.

The hunter lo'es the morning sun,
  To rouse the mountain deer, my jo ;
At noon the fisher takes the glen
  Adown the burn to steer, my jo :
Gie me the hour o' gloamin' gray,
  It maks my heart sae cheery O,
To meet thee on the lea-rig,
  My ain kind Dearie O.

O FOR ANE AN' TWENTY,
TAM

Chorus

An' O for ane an' twenty, Tam !
    And hey, sweet ane an' twenty, Tam !
I'll learn my kin a rattlin' sang,
    An' I saw ane an' twenty, Tam.

THEY snool me sair, and haud me doon,
    An' gar me look like bluntie, Tam ;
But three short years will soon wheel roon',
    An' then comes ane an' twenty, Tam.
        An' O for, etc.

A gleib o' lan', a claut o' gear,
    Was left me by my Auntie, Tam ;
At kith or kin I need na spier,
    An' I saw ane an' twenty, Tam.
        An' O for, etc.

They'll hae me wed a wealthy coof,
    Tho' I myself hae plenty, Tam ;
But hear'st thou, laddie ! there's my loof,
    I'm thine at ane an' twenty, Tam.
        An' O for, etc.

THOU FAIR ELIZA

Turn again, thou fair Eliza !
  Ae kind blink before we part ;
Rue on thy despairing lover,
  Canst thou break his faithfu' heart ?
Turn again, thou fair Eliza !
  If to love thy heart denies,
Oh, in pity hide the sentence
  Under friendship's kind disguise !

Thee, sweet maid, hae I offended ?
  My offence is loving thee ;
Canst thou wreck his peace for ever,
  Wha for thine would gladly die ?
While the life beats in my bosom,
  Thou shalt mix in ilka throe :
Turn again, thou lovely maiden,
  Ae sweet smile on me bestow.

Not the bee upon the blossom,
  In the pride o' sinny noon ;
Not the little sporting fairy,
  All beneath the simmer moon ;
Not the Minstrel, in the moment
  Fancy lightens in his e'e,
Kens the pleasure, feels the rapture,
  That thy presence gies to me.

C

CLARINDA, MISTRESS OF MY SOUL

CLARINDA, mistress of my soul,
　　The measur'd time is run !
The wretch beneath the dreary pole
　　So marks his latest sun.

To what dark cave of frozen night
　　Shall poor Sylvander hie ;
Depriv'd of thee, his life and light,
　　The sun of all his joy.

We part—but by these precious drops
　　That fill thy lovely eyes,
No other light shall guide my steps,
　　Till thy bright beams arise !

She, the fair sun of all her sex,
　　Has blest my glorious day ;
And shall a glimmering planet fix
　　My worship to its ray ?

FOR THE SAKE O' SOMEBODY

My heart is sair—I dare na tell,
  My heart is sair for Somebody ;
I could wake a winter night
  For the sake o' Somebody.
    O-hon ! for Somebody !
    O-hey ! for Somebody !
I could range the world around,
  For the sake o' Somebody.

Ye Powers that smile on virtuous love,
  O, sweetly smile on Somebody !
Frae ilka danger keep him free,
  And send me safe my Somebody !
    O-hon ! for Somebody !
    O-hey ! for Somebody !
I wad do—what wad I not ?
  For the sake o' Somebody.

NOW WESTLIN WINDS

Now westlin winds and slaught'ring guns
    Bring Autumn's pleasant weather ;
The moorcock springs on whirring wings,
    Amang the blooming heather :
Now waving grain, wide o'er the plain,
    Delights the weary farmer ;
And the moon shines bright, when I rove
    at night,
    To muse upon my charmer.

The partridge loves the fruitful fells,
    The plover loves the mountains ;
The woodcock haunts the lonely dells,
    The soaring hern the fountains :
Thro' lofty groves the cushat roves,
    The path of man to shun it ;
The hazel bush o'erhangs the thrush,
    The spreading thorn the linnet.

Thus ev'ry kind their pleasure find,
    The savage and the tender ;
Some social join, and leagues combine,
    Some solitary wander :
Avaunt, away, the cruel sway !
    Tyrannic man's dominion ;
The sportsman's joy, the murd'ring cry,
    The flutt'ring, gory pinion !

But, Peggy dear, the evening's clear,
  Thick flies the skimming swallow ;
The sky is blue, the fields in view,
  All fading-green and yellow :
Come let us stray our gladsome way,
  And view the charms of Nature ;
The rustling corn, the fruited thorn,
  And ev'ry happy creature.

We'll gently walk, and sweetly talk,
  Till the silent moon shine clearly ;
I'll grasp thy waist, and, fondly prest,
  Swear how I love thee dearly :
Not vernal show'rs to budding flow'rs,
  Not Autumn to the farmer,
So dear can be as thou to me,
  My fair, my lovely charmer !

A HEALTH TO ANE I LO'E DEAR

Chorus

Here's a health to ane I lo'e dear,
  Here's a health to ane I lo'e dear ;
Thou art sweet as the smile when fond lovers
    meet,
  And soft as their parting tear—Jessie.

ALTHO' thou maun never be mine,
  Altho' even hope is denied ;
'Tis sweeter for thee despairing,
  Than aught in the world beside—Jessie.
      Here's a health, etc.

I mourn thro' the gay, gaudy day,
  As hopeless I muse on thy charms ;
But welcome the dream o' sweet slumber,
  For then I am lockt in thine arms—Jessie.
      Here's a health, etc.

I guess by the dear angel smile,
  I guess by the love-rolling e'e ;
But why urge the tender confession,
  'Gainst Fortune's fell, cruel decree—Jessie.
      Here's a health, etc.

I'LL AY CA' IN BY YON TOWN

Chorus

I'll ay ca' in by yon town,
　　And by yon garden-green again ;
I'll ay ca' in by yon town,
　　And see my bonnie Jean again.

THERE's nane shall ken, there's nane can
　　guess
What brings me back the gate again,
But she, my fairest, faithfu' lass,
　　And stow'nlins we sall meet again.
　　　　　　I'll ca' ay in, etc.

She'll wander by the aiken tree,
　　When trystin' time draws near again ;
And when her lovely form I see,
　　O haith! she's doubly dear again.
　　　　　　I'll ay ca' in, etc.

A BOTTLE AND A FRIEND

Here's a bottle and an honest friend !
   What wad ye wish for mair, man ?
Wha kens, before his life may end,
   What his share may be o' care, man ?
Then catch the moments as they fly,
   And use them as ye ought, man :
Believe me, happiness is shy,
   And comes not aye when sought, man.

WILLIE BREW'D A PECK
O' MAUT

O Willie brew'd a peck o' maut,
   And Rob and Allan cam' to pree ;
Three blyther hearts, that lee-lang night,
   Ye wad na found in Christendie.

Chorus

We are na fou, we're nae that fou,
But just a drappie in our e'e ;
The cock may craw, the day may daw
   And ay we'll taste the barley bree.

Here are we met, three merry boys,
　　Three merry boys I trow are we ;
And mony a night we've merry been,
　　And mony mae we hope to be !
　　　　We are na fou, etc.

It is the moon, I ken her horn,
　　That's blinkin' in the lift sae hie ;
She shines sae bright to wyle us hame,
　　But, by my sooth, she'll wait a wee !
　　　　We are na fou, etc.

Wha first shall rise to gang awa',
　　A cuckold, coward loun is he !
Wha first beside his chair shall fa',
　　He is the King amang us three.
　　　　We are na fou, etc.

73

THE DEIL'S AWA' WI' TH' EXCISEMAN

THE deil cam fiddlin' thro' the town,
  And danc'd awa' wi' the Exciseman,
And ilka wife cries, ' Auld Mahoun,
  I wish you luck o' the prize, man.'

Chorus

The deil's awa', the deil's awa',
  The deil's awa' wi' th' Exciseman,
He's danc'd awa', he's danc'd awa',
  He's danc'd awa' wi' th' Exciseman.

We'll mak our maut, and we'll brew our drink,
  We'll laugh, sing, and rejoice, man,
And mony braw thanks to the meikle black deil,
  That danc'd awa' wi' th' Exciseman.
      The deil's awa', etc.

There's threesome reels, there's foursome reels,
  There's hornpipes and strathspeys, man,
But the ae best dance e'er cam to the land
  Was the deil's awa' wi' th' Exciseman.
      The deil's awa', etc.

MY LOVE, SHE'S BUT A
LASSIE YET

My love, she's but a lassie yet,
　My love, she's but a lassie yet ;
We'll let her stand a year or twa,
　She'll no be hauf sae saucy yet ;
I rue the day I sought her, O !
I rue the day I sought her, O !
Wha gets her need na say he's woo'd,
　But he may say he has bought her, O.

Come, draw a drap o' the best o't yet ;
　Come, draw a drap o' the best o't yet ;
Gae seek for pleasure whar you will,
　But here I never miss'd it yet,
We're a' dry wi' drinkin' o't ;
　We're a' dry wi' drinkin' o't ;
The minister kiss't the fiddler's wife ;
　He could na preach for thinkin' o't.

MY TOCHER'S THE JEWEL

O MEIKLE thinks my luve o' my beauty,
   And meikle thinks my luve o' my kin ;
But little thinks my luve I ken brawlie
   My tocher's the jewel has charms for him.
It's a' for the apple he'll nourish the tree,
   It's a' for the hiney he'll cherish the bee,
My laddie's sae meikle in luve wi' the siller,
   He canna hae luve to spare for me.

Your proffer o' luve's an airle-penny,
   My tocher's the bargain ye wad buy ;
But an' ye be crafty, I am cunnin',
   Sae ye wi' anither your fortune may try.
Ye're like to the timmer o' yon rotten wood,
   Ye're like to the bark o' yon rotten tree,
Ye'll slip frae me like a knotless thread,
   And ye'll crack your credit wi' mair nor me.

WHAT CAN A YOUNG LASSIE DO
WI' AN AULD MAN?

WHAT can a young lassie, what shall a young
    lassie,
  What can a young lassie do wi' an auld man?
Bad luck on the penny that tempted my
    minnie
  To sell her puir Jenny for siller an' lan' !
Bad luck on the penny that tempted my
    minnie
  To sell her puir Jenny for siller an' lan' !

He's always compleenin' frae mornin' to
    e'enin',
  He hoasts and he hirples the weary day lang ;
He's doylt and he's dozin', his blude it is
    frozen,—
  O dreary's the night wi' a crazy auld man !
He's doylt and he's dozin', his blude it is
    frozen,
  O dreary's the night wi' a crazy auld man.

He hums and he hankers, he frets and he
    cankers,
  I never can please him, do a' that I can ;

He's peevish an' jealous o' a' the young
    fellows,—
  O dool on the day I met wi' an auld man !
He's peevish an' jealous o' a' the young
    fellows,
  O dool on the day I met wi' an auld man.

My auld auntie Katie upon me taks pity,
  I'll do my endeavour to follow her plan ;
I'll cross him an' wrack him, until I heartbreak
    him,
    And then his auld brass 'll buy me a new
      pan !
I'll cross him an' wrack him, until I heartbreak
    him,
    And then his auld brass 'll buy me a new
      pan.

FAIREST MAID ON DEVON BANKS

Chorus
Fairest maid on Devon banks
    Crystal Devon, winding Devon,
Wilt thou lay that frown aside,
    And smile as thou wert wont to do?

FULL well thou know'st I love thee dear
Could thou to malice lend an ear ?
O did not Love exclaim, ' Forbear,
    Nor use a faithful lover so.'
                Fairest maid, etc.

Then come, thou fairest of the fair,
Those wonted smiles, O let me share ;
And by thy beauteous self I swear,
    No love but thine my heart shall know.
                Fairest maid, etc.

YOUNG JOCKEY WAS THE BLYTHEST LAD

Young Jockey was the blythest lad,
　In a' our town or here awa' ;
Fu' blythe he whistled at the gaud,
　Fu' lightly danc'd he in the ha' :

He roos'd my een sae bonnie blue,
　He roos'd my waist sae genty sma' ;
An' ay my heart cam to my mou',
　When ne'er a body heard or saw.

My Jockey toils upon the plain.
　Thro' wind and weet, thro' frost and
　　　snaw ;
And o'er the lea I leuk fu' fain,
　When Jockey's owsen hameward ca'.

An' ay the night comes round again,
　When in his arms he taks me a' ;
An' ay he vows he'll be my ain,
　As lang as he has breath to draw.

JOCKIE'S TAEN THE
PARTING KISS

Jockie's taen the parting kiss,
   O'er the mountain he is gane,
And with him is a' my bliss,
   Naught but griefs with me remain.
Spare my Love, ye winds that blaw,
   Plashy sleets and beating rain !
Spare my Love, thou feath'ry snaw,
   Drifting o'er the frozen plain !

When the shades of evening creep
   O'er the day's fair, gladsome e'e,
Sound and safely may he sleep,
   Sweetly blythe his waukening be.
He will think on her he loves,
   Fondly he'll repeat her name ;
For where'er he distant roves,
   Jockie's heart is still the same.

O WERE MY LOVE YON
LILAC FAIR

O WERE my love yon Lilac fair,
  Wi' purple blossoms to the Spring,
And I, a bird to shelter there,
  When wearied on my little wing !
How I wad mourn when it was torn
  By Autumn wild, and Winter rude !
But I wad sing on wanton wing,
  When youthfu' May its bloom renew'd.

O gin my love were yon red rose,
  That grows upon the castle wa' ;
And I mysel a drap o' dew,
  Into her bonnie breast to fa' !
O there, beyond expression blest,
  I'd feast on beauty a' the night ;
Seal'd on her silk-saft faulds to rest,
  Till fley'd awa' by Phœbus' light !

THOU HAST LEFT ME EVER,
JAMIE

Thou has left me ever, Jamie,
  Thou hast left me ever :
Thou hast left me ever, Jamie,
  Thou hast left me ever :
Aften hast thou vow'd that Death
  Only should us sever ;
Now thou'st left thy lass for ay—
  I maun see thee never, Jamie,
  I'll see thee never.

Thou hast me forsaken, Jamie,
  Thou hast me forsaken ;
Thou hast me forsaken, Jamie,
  Thou hast me forsaken ;
Thou canst love another jo,
  While my heart is breaking ;
Soon my weary een I'll close,
  Never mair to waken, Jamie,
  Never mair to waken !

MY CHLORIS, MARK HOW
GREEN THE GROVES

My Chloris ! mark how green the groves,
  The primrose banks how fair :
The balmy gales awake the flowers,
  And wave thy flaxen hair.
The lav'rock shuns the palace gay,
  And o'er the cottage sings ;
For nature smiles as sweet, I ween,
  To shepherds as to kings.

Let minstrels sweep the skilfu' string
  In lordly lighted ha' ;
The shepherd stops his simple reed,
  Blythe, in the birken shaw :
The princely revel may survey
  Our rustic dance wi' scorn ;
But are their hearts as light as ours
  Beneath the milk-white thorn ?

The shepherd, in the flowery glen,
  In shepherd's phrase will woo ;
The courtier tells a finer tale ;
  But is his heart as true ?
These wild-wood flowers I've pu'd, to deck
  That spotless breast o' thine :
The courtier's gems may witness love—
  But 'tis na love lik. mine.

'TWAS NA HER BONNIE BLUE E'E

'Twas na her bonnie blue e'e was my ruin,
Fair tho's she be, that was ne'er my undoin';
'Twas the dear smile when naebody did mind
    us,
'Twas the bewitching, sweet, stown glance o'
    kindness,
'Twas the bewitching, sweet, stown glance o'
    kindness.

Sair do I fear that to hope is denied me,
Sair do I fear that despair maun abide me,
But tho' fell fortune should fate us to sever,
Queen shall she be in my bosom for ever :
Queen shall she be in my bosom for ever.

Chloris, I'm thine wi' a passion sincerest,
And thou hast plighted me love o' the dearest !
And thou'rt the angel that never can alter,
Sooner the sun in his motion would falter :
Sooner the sun in his motion would falter.

ADDRESS TO THE WOODLARK

O STAY, sweet warbling woodlark, stay,
Nor quit for me the trembling spray,
A hapless lover courts thy lay,
   Thy soothing, fond complaining.
Again, again that tender part,
That I may catch thy melting art ;
For surely that wad touch her heart
   Wha kills me wi' disdaining.

Say, was thy little mate unkind,
And heard thee as the careless wind ?
Oh, nocht but love and sorrow join'd,
   Sic notes o' woe could wauken !
Thou tells o' never-ending care ;
O' speechless grief, and dark despair :
For pity's sake, sweet bird, nae mair !
   Or my poor heart is broken.

HOW CRUEL ARE THE PARENTS

(Altered from an old English song)

How cruel are the parents
　Who riches only prize,
And to the wealthy booby
　Poor Woman sacrifice !
Meanwhile, the hapless Daughter
　Has but a choice of strife ;
To shun a tyrant Father's hate—
　Become a wretched wife.

The ravening hawk pursuing,
　The trembling dove thus flies,
To shun impelling ruin,
　Awhile her pinions tries;
Till, of escape despairing,
　No shelter or retreat,
She trusts the ruthless Falconer,
　And drops beneath his feet.

JOHN BARLEYCORN

(*A Ballad*)

THERE was three kings into the east,
   Three kings both great and high,
And they hae sworn a solemn oath
   John Barleycorn should die.

They took a plough and plough'd him
     down,
   Put clods upon his head,
And they hae sworn a solemn oath
   John Barleycorn was dead.

But the cheerful Spring came kindly on,
   And show'rs began to fall ;
John Barleycorn got up again,
   And sore surpris'd them all.

The sultry suns of Summer came,
   And he grew thick and strong ;
His head weel arm'd wi' pointed spears,
   That no one should him wrong.

The sober Autumn enter'd mild,
   When he grew wan and pale ;
His bending joints and drooping head
   Show'd he began to fail.

His colour sicken'd more and more,
 He faded into age ;
And then his enemies began
 To show their deadly rage.

They've taen a weapon, long and sharp,
 And cut him by the knee ;
Then ty'd him fast upon a cart,
 Like a rogue for forgerie.

They laid him down upon his back,
 And cudgell'd him full sore ;
They hung him up before the storm,
 And turn'd him o'er and o'er.

They fillèd up a darksome pit
 With water to the brim,
They heavèd in John Barleycorn—
 There, let him sink or swim.

They laid him out upon the floor,
 To work him farther woe ;
And still, as signs of life appear'd,
 They toss'd him to and fro.

They wasted, o'er a scorching flame,
 The marrow of his bones ;
But a miller us'd him worst of all,
 For he crush'd him between two stones.

And they hae taen his very heart's blood,
  And drank it round and round ;
And still the more and more they drank,
  Their joy did more abound.

John Barleycorn was a hero bold,
  Of noble enterprise ;
For if you do but taste his blood,
  'Twill make your courage rise.

'Twill make a man forget his woe ;
  'Twill heighten all his joy :
'Twill make the widow's heart to sing,
  Tho' the tear were in her eye.

Then let us toast John Barleycorn,
  Each man a glass in hand ;
And may his great posterity
  Ne'er fail in old Scotland !

THE SODGER'S RETURN

WHEN wild war's deadly blast was
    blawn
  And gentle peace returning,
Wi' mony a sweet babe fatherless,
  And mony a widow mourning ;
I left the lines and tented field,
  Where lang I'd been a lodger,
My humble knapsack a' my wealth,
  A poor but honest sodger.

A leal, light heart was in my breast,
  My hand unstain'd wi' plunder ;
And for fair Scotia, hame again,
  I cheery on did wander :
I thought upon the banks o' Coil,
  I thought upon my Nancy,
I thought upon the witching smile
  That caught my youthful fancy.

At length I reach'd the bonnie glen,
  Where early life I sported ;
I pass'd the mill and trysting thorn,
  Where Nancy aft I courted :
Wha spied I but my ain dear maid,
  Down by her mother's dwelling !
And turn'd me round to hide the flood
  That in my een was swelling.

Wi' alter'd voice, quoth I, Sweet lass,
    Sweet as yon hawthorn's blossom,
O! happy, happy may he be,
    That's dearest to thy bosom :
My purse is light, I've far to gang,
    And fain would be thy lodger ;
I've served my king and country lang—
    Take pity on a sodger.

Sae wistfully she gaz'd on me,
    And lovelier was than ever ;
Quo' she, a sodger ance I lo'ed,
    Forget him shall I never :
Our humble cot, and hamely fare,
    Ye freely shall partake it ;
That gallant badge—the dear cockade,
    Ye're welcome for the sake o't.

She gaz'd—she redden'd like a rose—
    Syne pale like ony lily ;
She sank within my arms, and cried,
    Art thou my ain dear Willie ?
By Him who made yon sun and sky !
    By whom true love's regarded,
I am the man ; and thus may still
    True lovers be rewarded !

The wars are o'er, and I'm come hame,
    And find thee still true-hearted ;

Tho' poor in gear, we're rich in love,
    And mair we'se ne'er be parted.
Quo' she, My grandsire left me gowd,
    A mailen plenish'd fairly ;
And come, my faithfu' sodger lad,
    Thou'rt welcome to it dearly !

For gold the merchant ploughs the main,
    The farmer ploughs the manor :
But glory is the sodger's prize,
    The sodger's wealth is honour :
The brave poor sodger ne'er despise,
    Nor count him as a stranger ;
Remember he's his country's stay,
    In day and hour of danger.

THE BRAW WOOER

Last May a braw wooer cam doun the lang
glen,
　And sair wi' his love he did deave me ;
I said there was naething I hated like men—
　The deuce gae wi'm, to believe me, believe
me ;
　The deuce gae wi'm to believe me.

He spake o' the darts in my bonnie black een,
　And vow'd for my love he was diein',
I said he might die when he liket—for Jean—
　The Lord forgie me for liein', for liein' ;
　The Lord forgie me for liein' !

A weel-stocket mailen, himself for the laird,
　And marriage aff-hand, were his proffers ;
I never loot on that I kenn'd it, or car'd,
　But thought I might hae waur offers, waur
offers ;
　But thought I might hae waur offers.

But what wad ye think ?—in a fortnight or
less—
　The deil tak his taste to gae near her !
He up the *Gate-slack* to my black cousin, Bess—
　Guess ye how, the jad ! I could bear her,
could bear her ;
　Guess ye how, the jad ! I could bear her.

94

But a' the neist week, as I petted wi' care,
  I gaed to the tryst o' Dalgarnock ;
And wha but my fine fickle wooer was there,
  I glowr'd as I'd seen a warlock, a warlock,
  I glowr'd as I'd seen a warlock.

But owre my left shouther I gae him a blink,
  Lest neibours might say I was saucy ;
My wooer he caper'd as he'd been in drink,
  And vow'd I was his dear lassie, dear lassie,
  And vow'd I was his dear lassie.

I spier'd for my cousin fu' couthy and sweet,
  Gin she had recover'd her hearin',
And how her new shoon fit her auld shachl't
    feet,
  But heavens ! how he fell a swearin', a
    swearin',
  But heavens! how he fell a swearin'.

He begged, for gudesake, I wad be his wife,
  Or else I wad kill him wi' sorrow ;
So e'en to preserve the poor body in life,
  I think I maun wed him to-morrow, to-
    morrow ;
  I think I maun wed him to-morrow.

BONNIE JEAN

THERE was a lass, and she was fair,
　At kirk and market to be seen ;
When a' our fairest maids were met,
　The fairest maid was bonnie Jean.

And ay she wrought her mammie's wark,
　And ay she sang sae merrilie ;
The blythest bird upon the bush
　Had ne'er a lighter heart than she.

But hawks will rob the tender joys
　That bless the little lintwhite's nest ;
And frost will blight the fairest flowers,
　And love will break the soundest rest.

Young Robie was the brawest lad,
　The flower and pride of a' the glen ;
And he had owsen, sheep, and kye,
　And wanton naigies nine or ten.

He gaed wi' Jeanie to the tryste,
　He danc'd wi' Jeanie on the down ;
And, lang ere witless Jeanie wist,
　Her heart was tint, her peace was stown !

As in the bosom of the stream,
   The moonbeam dwells at dewy e'en ;
So trembling, pure, was tender love
   Within the breast of bonnie Jean.

And now she works her mammie's wark,
   And ay she sighs wi' care and pain ;
Ye wist na what her ail might be,
   Or what wad make her weel again.

But did na Jeanie's heart loup light,
   And did na joy blink in her e'e ;
As Robie tauld a tale of love :
   Ae e'enin' on the lily lea ?

The sun was sinking in the west,
   The birds sang sweet in ilka grove ;
His cheeks to hers he fondly laid,
   And whisper'd thus his tale o' love :

O Jeanie fair, I lo'e thee dear ;
   O canst thou think to fancy me,
Or wilt thou leave thy mammie's cot,
   And learn to tent the farms wi' me ?

At barn or byre thou shalt na drudge,
   Or naething else to trouble thee ;
But stray amang the heather-bells,
   And tent the waving corn wi' me.

D

Now what could artless Jeanie do ?
　She had na will to say him na :
At length she blush'd a sweet consent,
　And love was ay between them twa.

THE COUNTRY LASSIE

In simmer, when the hay was mawn,
　And corn wav'd green in ilka field,
While claver blooms white o'er the lea
　And roses blaw in ilka bield !
Blythe Bessie in the milking shiel,
　Says—I'll be wed, come o't what will
Out spake a dame in wrinkled eild—
　O' gude advisement comes nae ill.

It's ye hae wooers mony ane,
　And lassie ye're but young, ye ken ;
Then wait a wee, and cannie wale
　A routhie butt, a routhie ben ;
There's Johnny o' the Buskie-glen,
　Fu' is his barn, fu' is his byre ;
Tak this frae me, my bonnie hen,
　It's plenty beets the luver's fire.

For Johnny o' the Buskie-glen,
    I dinna care a single flie ;
He lo'es sae well his craps and kye,
    He has nae luve to spare for me ;
But blythe the blink o' Robie's e'e,
    And weel I wat he lo'es me dear ;
Ae blink o' him I wad na gie
    For Buskie-glen and a' his gear.

O thoughtless lassie, life's a faught ;
    The canniest gate, the strife is sair ;
But ay fu'-han't is fechtin' best,
    A hungry care's an unco care :
But some will spend and some will spare,
    An' wilfu' folk maun hae their will ;
Syne as ye brew, my maiden fair,
    Keep mind that ye maun drink the yill.

O gear will buy me rigs o' land,
    And gear will buy me sheep and kye ;
But the tender heart o' leesome luve,
    The gowd and siller canna buy ;
We may be poor—Robie and I—
    Light is the burden luve lays on ;
Content and luve brings peace and joy—
    What mair hae Queens upon a throne ?

MY NANIE, O

BEHIND yon hills where Lugar flows,
　'Mang moors an' mosses many, O,
The wintry sun the day has clos'd,
　And I'll awa' to Nanie, O.

The westlin wind blaws loud an' shill ;
　The night's baith mirk and rainy, O :
But I'll get my plaid an' out I'll steal,
　An' owre the hill to Nanie, O.

My Nanie's charming, sweet, an' young ;
　Nae artfu' wiles to win ye, O :
May ill befa' the flattering tongue
　That wad beguile my Nanie, O.

Her face is fair, her heart is true ;
　As spotless as she's bonnie, O ;
The op'ning gowan, wat wi' dew,
　Nae purer is than Nanie, O.

A country lad is my degree,
　An' few there be that ken me, O ;
But what care I how few they be,
　I'm welcome ay to Nanie, O.

My riches a's my penny-fee,
  An' I maun guide it cannie, O,
But warl's gear ne'er troubles me,
  My thoughts are a'—my Nanie, O.

Our auld guidman delights to view
  His sheep an' kye thrive bonnie, O ;
But I'm as blythe that hauds his pleugh
  An' has nae care but Nanie, O.

Come weel, come woe, I care na by ;
  I'll tak what Heav'n will sen' me, O ;
Nae ither care in life have I,
  But live, an' love my Nanie, O.

DUNCAN DAVIDSON

THERE was a lass, they ca'd her Meg,
  And she held o'er the moors to spin ;
There was a lad that follow'd her,
  They ca'd him Duncan Davidson.
The moon was dreigh, and Meg was skeigh,
  Her favour Duncan could na win ;
For wi' the rock she wad him knock,
  And ay she shook the temper-pin.

As o'er the moor they lightly foor,
  A burn was clear, a glen was green ;
Upon the banks they eas'd their shanks,
  And ay she set the wheel between :
But Duncan swoor a haly aith,
  That Meg should be a bride the morn ;
Then Meg took up her spinnin'-graith,
  And flang them a' out o'er the burn.

We will big a wee, wee house,
  And we will live like king and queen ;
Sae blythe and merry 's we will be,
  When ye set by the wheel at e'en.
A man may drink, and no be drunk ;
  A man may fight and no be slain ;
A man may kiss a bonnie lass,
  And ay be welcome back again !

WHISTLE O'ER THE LAVE O'T

FIRST when Maggie was my care,
Heav'n, I thought, was in her air,
Now we're married—spier nae mair,
  But whistle o'er the lave o't !

Meg was meek, and Meg was mild,
Sweet and harmless as a child—
Wiser men than me's beguil'd ;
  Whistle o'er the lave o't !

How we live, my Meg and me,
How we love, and how we gree,
I care na by how few may see—
  Whistle o'er the lave o't !

Wha I wish were maggot's meat,
Dish'd up in her winding-sheet,
I could write—but Meg may see't—
  Whistle o'er the lave o't !

DAINTY DAVIE

Now rosy May comes in wi' flowers,
To deck her gay, green-spreading bowers ;
And now comes in the happy hours,
　　To wander wi' my Davie.

Chorus
Meet me on the warlock knowe,
　　Dainty Davie, dainty Davie ;
There I'll spend the day wi' you,
　　My ain dear, dainty Davie.

The crystal waters round us fa',
The merry birds are lovers a',
The scented breezes round us blaw,
　　A-wandering wi' my Davie.
　　　　　　Meet me on, etc.

As purple morning starts the hare,
To steal upon her early fare,
Then thro' the dews I will repair,
　　To meet my faithfu' Davie.
　　　　　　Meet me on, etc.

When day, expiring in the west,
The curtain draws o' Nature's rest,
I flee to his arms I lo'e the best,
　　And that's my ain dear Davie.
　　　　　　Meet me on, etc.

THE GALLANT WEAVER

WHERE Cart rins rowin' to the sea,
By mony a flower and spreading tree,
There lives a lad, the lad for me,
    He is a gallant Weaver.
O I had wooers aught or nine,
They gied me rings and ribbons fine ;
And I was fear'd my heart wad tine,
    And I gied it to the Weaver.

My daddie sign'd my tocher-band,
To gie the lad that has the land,
But to my heart I'll add my hand,
    And give it to the Weaver.
While birds rejoice in leafy bowers,
While bees delight in opening flowers,
While corn grows green in summer showers,
    I'll love my gallant Weaver.

ANNA, THY CHARMS

ANNA, thy charms my bosom fire,
  And waste my soul with care ;
But ah ! how bootless to admire,
  When fated to despair !

Yet in thy presence, lovely fair,
  To hope may be forgiven ;
For sure, 'twere impious to despair
  So much in sight of heaven.

NOW SPRING HAS CLAD THE
GROVE IN GREEN

Now Spring has clad the grove in green,
  And strew'd the lea wi' flowers ;
The furrow'd, waving corn is seen
  Rejoice in fostering showers.
While ilka thing in nature join
  Their sorrows to forego,
O why thus all alone are mine
  The weary steps o' woe !

The trout in yonder wimplin' burn
  That glides—a silver dart,
And, safe beneath the shady thorn
  Defies the angler's art ;
My life was ance that careless stream,
  That wanton trout was I ;
But Love, wi' unrelenting beam,
  Has scorch'd my fountains dry.

That little floweret's peaceful lot,
  In yonder cliff that grows,
Which, save the linnet's flight, I wot,
  Nae ruder visit knows,
Was mine, till Love has o'er me past,
  And blighted a' my bloom ;
And now, beneath the withering blast,
  My youth and joy consume.

The waken'd lav'rock warbling springs,
    And climbs the early sky,
Winnowing blythe his dewy wings
    In morning's rosy eye ;
As little reck'd I sorrow's power,
    Until the flowery snare
O' witching Love, in luckless hour,
    Made me the thrall o' care.

O had my fate been Greenland snows,
    Or Afric's burning zone,
Wi' man and nature leagu'd my foes,
    So Peggy ne'er I'd known !
The wretch whose doom is ' hope nae
        mair,'
    What tongue his woes can tell ;
Within whase bosom, save Despair,
    Nae kinder spirits dwell.

A LASS WI' A TOCHER

Awa' wi' your witchcraft o' Beauty's alarms,
The slender bit Beauty you grasp in your arms,
O, gie me the lass that has acres o' charms,
O' gie me the lass wi' the weel-stockit farms.

Chorus
Then hey, for a lass wi' a tocher,
Then hey, for a lass wi' a tocher ;
Then hey, for a lass wi' a tocher ;
The nice yellow guineas for me.

Your Beauty's a flower, in the morning that
blows,
And withers the faster, the faster it grows :
But the rapturous charm o' the bonnie green
knowes,
Ilk spring they're new deckit wi' bonnie white
yowes.
Then hey for a lass, etc.

And e'en when this Beauty your bosom hath
blest,
The brightest o' Beauty may cloy when
possess'd ;
But the sweet, yellow darlings wi' Geordie
impress'd,
The langer ye hae them, the mair they're carest.
Then hey for a lass, etc.

MALLY'S MEEK, MALLY'S SWEET

Chorus
Mally's meek, Mally's sweet,
Mally's modest and discreet ;
Mally's rare, Mally's fair,
   Mally's every way complete.

As I was walking up the street,
  A barefit maid I chanc'd to meet ;
But O the road was very hard
  For that fair maiden's tender feet.
     Mally's meek, etc.

It were mair meet that those fine feet
  Were weel laced up in silken shoon ;
An' 'twere more fit that she should sit
  Within yon chariot gilt aboon.
     Mally's meek, etc.

Her yellow hair, beyond compare,
  Comes trinklin' down her swan-like neck,
And her two eyes, like stars in skies,
  Would keep a sinking ship frae wreck.
     Mally's meek, etc.

WAT YE WHA'S IN YON TOWN?

Chorus

O wat ye wha's in yon town,
　　Ye see the e'enin' sun upon?
The dearest maid's in yon town,
　　That e'enin' sun is shining on.

Now haply down yon gay green shaw,
　　She wanders by yon spreading tree;
How blest ye flowers that round her
　　　blaw,
　　Ye catch the glances o' her e'e!
　　　　O wat ye wha's, etc.

How blest ye birds that round her sing,
　　And welcome in the blooming year;
And doubly welcome be the Spring,
　　The season to my Jeanie dear.
　　　　O wat ye wha's, etc.

The sun blinks blythe in yon town,
　　Among the broomy braes sae green;
But my delight in yon town,
　　And dearest pleasure, is my Jean.
　　　　O wat ye wha's, etc.

Without my Fair, not a' the charms
    O' Paradise could yield me joy ;
But give me Jeanie in my arms,
    And welcome Lapland's dreary sky !
        O wat ye wha's, etc.

My cave wad be a lover's bower,
    Tho' raging Winter rent the air ;
And she a lovely little flower,
    That I wad tent and shelter there.
        O wat ye wha's, etc.

O sweet is she in yon town,
    The sinkin' Sun's gane down upon ;
A fairer than's in yon town,
    His setting beam ne'er shone upon.
        O wat ye wha's, etc.

If angry Fate is sworn my foe,
    And suff'ring I am doom'd to bear ;
I careless quit aught else below,
    But spare, O spare me Jeanie dear.
        O wat ye wha's, etc.

For while life's dearest blood is warm,
    Ae thought frae her shall ne'er depart,
And she, as fairest is her form,
    She has the truest, kindest heart.
        O wat ye wha's, etc.

SWEET FA'S THE EVE

Sweet fa's the eve on Craigie-burn,
    And blythe awakes the morrow,
But a' the pride o' spring's return
    Can yield me nocht but sorrow.

I see the flowers and spreading trees,
    I hear the wild birds singing ;
But what a weary wight can please,
    And care his bosom wringing ?

Fain, fain would I my griefs impart,
    Yet dare na for your anger ;
But secret love will break my heart,
    If I conceal it langer.

If thou refuse to pity me,
    If thou shalt love anither,
When yon green leaves fa' frae the tree,
    Around my grave they'll wither.

THEIR GROVES O' SWEET MYRTLE

THEIR groves o' sweet myrtle let Foreign
    Lands reckon,
  Where bright beaming summers exalt the
    perfume ;
Far dearer to me yon lone glen o' green
    breckan,
  Wi' the burn stealing under the lang, yellow
    broom.
Far dearer to me are yon humble broom
    bowers,
  Where the blue-bell and gowan lurk, lowly,
    unseen :
For there, lightly tripping, among the wild
    flowers,
  A-list'ning the linnet, aft wanders my
    Jean.

Tho' rich is the breeze in their gay, sunny
    valleys,
  And cauld Caledonia's blast on the
    wave ;
Their sweet-scented woodlands that skirt the
    proud palace,
  What are they ?—the haunt of the Tyrant
    and Slave.

The Slave's spicy forests, and gold-bubbling
    fountains,
    The brave Caledonian views with disdain ;
He wanders as free as the winds of his moun-
    tains,
    Save Love's willing fetters—the chains o' his
    Jean.

BONNIE WEE THING

Chorus

Bonnie wee thing, cannie wee thing,
    Lovely wee thing, wert thou mine,
I wad wear thee in my bosom,
    Lest my jewel it should tine.

Wishfully I look and languish
    In that bonnie face o' thine,
And my heart it stounds wi' anguish,
    Lest my wee thing be na mine.
        Bonnie wee thing, etc.

Wit and Grace, and Love, and Beauty,
    In ae constellation shine ;
To adore thee is my duty,
    Goddess o' this soul o' mine !
        Bonnie wee thing, etc.

I HAE A WIFE O' MY AIN

I HAE a wife o' my ain,
  I'll partake wi' naebody;
I'll take cuckold frae nane,
  I'll gie cuckold to naebody.

I hae a penny to spend,
  There—thanks to naebody!
I hae naething to lend,
  I'll borrow frae naebody.

I am naebody's lord,
  I'll be slave to naebody;
I hae a gude braid sword,
  I'll tak dunts frae naebody.

I'll be merry and free,
  I'll be sad for naebody;
Naebody cares for me,
  I care for naebody.

MY WIFE'S A WINSOME
WEE THING

Chorus

She is a winsome wee thing,
She is a handsome wee thing,
She is a lo'esome wee thing,
   This dear wee wife o' mine.

I NEVER saw a fairer,
I never lo'ed a dearer,
And neist my heart I'll wear her,
  For fear my jewel tine.
     She is a winsome, etc.

The warld's wrack we share o't ;
The warstle and the care o't ;
Wi' her I'll blythely bear it,
  And think my lot divine.
     She is a winsome, etc.

THE LASS O' BALLOCHMYLE

'TWAS even—the dewy fields were green,
　　On every blade the pearls hang ;
The zephyr wanton'd round the bean,
　　And bore its fragrant sweets alang :
In ev'ry glen the mavis sang,
　　All nature list'ning seem'd the while,
Except where greenwood echoes rang,
　　Amang the braes o' Ballochmyle.

With careless step I onward stray'd,
　　My heart rejoic'd in nature's joy,
When, musing in a lonely glade,
　　A maiden fair I chanc'd to spy :
Her look was like the morning's eye,
　　Her air like nature's vernal smile ;
Perfection whisper'd, passing by,
　　" Behold the lass o' Ballochmyle ! '

Fair is the morn in flowery May,
　　And sweet is night in autumn mild ;
When roving thro' the garden gay,
　　Or wand'ring in the lonely wild :
But woman, nature's darling child !
　　There all her charms she does compile ;
Even there her other works are foil'd
　　By the bonnie lass o' Ballochmyle.

O had she been a country maid,
   And I the happy country swain,
Tho' shelter'd in the lowest shed
   That ever rose on Scotland's plain !
Thro' weary winter's wind and rain,
   With joy, with rapture, I would toil ;
And nightly to my bosom strain
   The bonnie lass o' Ballochmyle.

Then pride might climb the slipp'ry steep,
   Where fame and honours lofty shine ;
And thirst of gold might tempt the deep,
   Or downward seek the Indian mine :
Give me the cot below the pine,
   To tend the flocks or till the soil ;
And ev'ry day have joys divine
   With the bonnie lass o' Ballochmyle.

LASSIE WI' THE LINT-WHITE LOCKS

Chorus

Lassie wi' the lint-white locks,
    Bonnie lassie, artless lassie,
Wilt thou wi' me tent the flocks,
    Wilt thou be my Dearie, O ?

Now Nature cleeds the flowery lea,
And a' is young and sweet like thee,
O wilt thou share its joys wi' me,
    And say thou'lt be my Dearie, O ?
        Lassie wi' the, etc.

The primrose bank, the wimpling burn,
The cuckoo on the milk-white thorn,
The wanton lambs at early morn,
    Shall welcome thee, my Dearie, O.
        Lassie wi' the, etc.

And when the welcome summer shower
Has cheer'd ilk drooping little flower,
We'll to the breathing woodbine-bower,
    At sultry noon, my Dearie, O.
        Lassie wi' the, etc.

When Cynthia lights, wi' silver ray,
The weary shearer's hameward way,
Thro' yellow waving fields we'll stray,
    And talk o' love, my Dearie, O.
            Lassie wi' the, etc.

And when the howling wintry blast
Disturbs my lassie's midnight rest,
Enclaspèd to my faithfu' breast,
    I'll comfort thee, my Dearie, O.
            Lassie wi' the, etc.

WILT THOU BE MY DEARIE?

WILT thou be my Dearie?
When sorrow wrings thy gentle heart.
    O wilt thou let me cheer thee !
By the treasure of my soul,
    That's the love I bear thee :
I swear and vow that only thou
    Shall ever be my Dearie !
Only thou, I swear and vow,
    Shall ever be my Dearie !

    Lassie, say thou lo'es me ;
Or, if thou wilt na be my ain,
    O say na thou'lt refuse me !
If it winna, canna be,
    Thou for thine may choose me,
Let me, lassie, quickly die,
    Still trusting that thou lo'es me !
Lassie, let me quickly die,
    Still trusting that thou lo'es me !

OUT OVER THE FORTH

Out over the Forth I look to the north,
  But what is the north and its Highlands to
    me ?
The south nor the east gie ease to my breast,
  The far foreign land, or the wild rolling sea.

But I look to the west, when I gae to rest,
  That happy my dreams and my slumbers
    may be ;
For far in the west lives he I lo'e best,
  The lad that is dear to my babie and me.

POEM ON SENSIBILITY

Sᴇɴꜱɪʙɪʟɪᴛʏ, how charming,
　Dearest Nancy, thou canst tell ;
But distress, with horrors arming,
　Thou alas ! hast known too well !

Fairest flower, behold the lily
　Blooming in the sunny ray ;
Let the blast sweep o'er the valley,
　See it prostrate in the clay.

Hear the woodlark charm the forest,
　Telling o'er his little joys ;
But alas ! a prey the surest
　To each pirate of the skies.

Dearly bought the hidden treasure
　Finer feelings can bestow :
Chords that vibrate sweetest pleasure
　Thrill the deepest notes of woe.

ON A BANK OF FLOWERS

On a bank of flowers in a summer day,
  For summer lightly drest,
The youthful, blooming Nelly lay,
  With love and sleep opprest ;

When Willie, wand'ring thro' the wood,
Who for her favour oft had sued ;
    He gaz'd, he wish'd,
    He fear'd, he blush'd,
And trembled where he stood.

Her closèd eyes, like weapons sheath'd,
  Were seal'd in soft repose ;
Her lips, still as she fragrant breath'd,
  It richer dyed the rose ;

The springing lilies, sweetly prest,
Wild-wanton kiss'd her rival breast ;
    He gaz'd, he wish'd,
    He fear'd, he blush'd,
His bosom ill at rest.

Her robes light-waving in the breeze,
  Her tender limbs embrace ;
Her lovely form, her native ease,
  All harmony and grace ;

Tumultuous tides his pulses roll,
A faltering, ardent kiss he stole ;
  He gaz'd, he wish'd,
  He fear'd, he blush'd,
And sigh'd his very soul.

As flies the partridge from the brake,
 On fear-inspirèd wings,
So Nelly, starting, half-awake,
 Away affrighted springs ;

But Willie follow'd—as he should,
He overtook her in the wood ;
  He vow'd, he pray'd,
  He found the maid
Forgiving all and good.

YOUNG PEGGY

Young Peggy blooms our bonniest lass,
   Her blush is like the morning,
The rosy dawn, the springing grass,
   With early gems adorning.
Her eyes outshine the radiant beams
   That gild the passing shower,
And glitter o'er the crystal streams,
   And cheer each fresh'ning flower.

Her lips, more than the cherries bright,
   A richer dye has graced them ;
They charm th' admiring gazer's sight,
   And sweetly tempt to taste them ;
Her smile is as the evening mild,
   When feather'd pairs are courting,
And little lambkins wanton wild,
   In playful bands disporting.

Were Fortune lovely Peggy's foe,
   Such sweetness would relent her ;
As blooming spring unbends the brow
   Of surly savage winter.
Detraction's eye no aim can gain,
   Her winning pow'rs to lessen ;
And fretful Envy grins in vain
   The poison'd tooth to fasten.

Ye Pow'rs of Honour, Love and Truth
  From ev'ry ill defend her !
Inspire the highly-favour'd youth
  The destinies intend her :
Still fan the sweet connubial flame
  Responsive in each bosom ;
And bless the dear parental name
  With many a filial blossom.

THE LASS OF CESSNOCK BANKS

On Cessnock banks a lassie dwells ;
  Could I describe her shape and mien ;
Our lasses a' she far excels,
  An' she has twa sparkling rogueish een.

She's sweeter than the morning dawn,
  When rising Phœbus first is seen ;
And dew-drops twinkle o'er the lawn ;
  An' she has twa sparkling rogueish een.

She's stately like yon youthful ash,
  That grows the cowslip braes between,
And drinks the stream with vigour fresh ;
  An' she has twa sparkling rogueish een.

She's spotless like the flow'ring thorn,
  With flow'rs so white and leaves so green,
When purest in the dewy morn ;
  An' she has twa sparkling rogueish een.

Her looks are like the vernal May,
  When ev'ning Phœbus shines serene ;
While birds rejoice on every spray ;
  An' she has twa sparkling rogueish een.

Her hair is like the curling mist,
    That climbs the mountain-sides at e'en,
When flow'r-reviving rains are past ;
    An' she has twa sparkling rogueish een.

Her forehead's like the show'ry bow,
    When gleaming sunbeams intervene
And gild the distant mountain's brow ;
    An' she has twa sparkling rogueish een.

Her cheeks are like yon crimson gem,
    The pride of all the flowery scene,
Just opening on its thorny stem ;
    An' she has twa sparkling rogueish een.

Her bosom's like the nightly snow,
    When pale the morning rises keen ;
While hid the murm'ring streamlets flow ;
    An' she has twa sparkling rogueish een.

Her lips are like yon cherries ripe,
    That sunny walls from Boreas screen ;
They tempt the taste and charm the sight ;
    An' she has twa sparkling rogueish een.

Her teeth are like a flock of sheep,
    With fleeces newly washen clean ;
That slowly mount the rising steep ;
    An' she has twa sparkling rogueish een.

Her breath is like the fragrant breeze,
  That gently stirs the blossom'd bean ;
When Phœbus sinks behind the seas ;
  An' she has twa sparkling rogueish een.

Her voice is like the ev'ning thrush,
  That sings on Cessnock banks unseen ;
While his mate sits nestling in the bush ;
  An' she has twa sparkling rogueish een.

But it's not her air, her form, her face,
  Tho' matching beauty's fabled queen ;
'Tis the mind that shines in ev'ry grace.
  An' chiefly in her rogueish een.

I'M O'ER YOUNG TO MARRY YET

Chorus

I'm o'er young, I'm o'er young,
  I'm o'er young to marry yet ;
I'm o'er young, 'twad be a sin
  To tak me frae my mammy yet.

I AM my mammy's ae bairn,
  Wi' unco folk I weary, sir ;
And lying in a strange bed,
  I'm fley'd it mak me eerie, sir.
      I'm o'er young, etc.

Hallowmass is come and gane,
  The nights are lang in winter, sir,
And you an' I in ae bed,
  In trowth, I dare na venture, sir.
      I'm o'er young, etc.

Fu' loud an' shill the frosty wind
  Blaws thro' the leafless timmer, sir ;
But if ye come this gate again,
  I'll aulder be gin simmer, sir.
      I'm o'er young, etc.

ROBIN SHURE IN HAIRST

ROBIN shure in hairst,
  I shure wi' him ;
Fient a heuk had I,
  Yet I stack by him.

I gaed up to Dunse,
  To warp a wab o' plaiden ;
At his daddie's yett,
  Wha met me but Robin ?

Was na Robin bauld,
  Tho' I was a cotter,
Play'd me sick a trick
  And me the eller's dochter ?

Robin promis'd me
  A' my winter vittle ;
Fient haet he had but three
  Goose feathers and a whittle.

BANNOCKS O' BARLEY

Bannocks o' bear meal,
  Bannocks o' barley;
Here's to the Highlandman's
  Bannocks o' barley.
Wha in a brulzie
  Will first cry a parley?
Never the lads wi'
  The bannocks o' barley.

Bannocks o' bear meal,
  Bannocks o' barley;
Here's to the lads wi'
  The bannocks o' barley;
Wha in his wae-days
  Were loyal to Charlie?
Wha but the lads wi'
  The bannocks o' barley.

COMIN' THRO' THE RYE

Chorus

O Jenny's a' weet, poor body,
  Jenny's seldom dry ;
She draigl't a' her petticoatie,
  Comin' thro' the rye.

COMIN' thro' the rye, poor body,
  Comin' thro' the rye,
She draigl't a' her petticoatie,
  Comin' thro' the rye.

Gin a body meet a body
  Comin' thro' the rye,
Gin a body kiss a body,
  Need a body cry ?

Gin a body meet a body
  Comin' thro' the glen,
Gin a body kiss a body,
  Need the warld ken ?

Chorus

O Jenny's a' weet, poor body,
  Jenny's seldom dry ;
She draigl't a' her petticoatie,
  Comin' thro' the rye.

THE LASS O' ECCLEFECHAN

Gat ye me, O gat ye me,
  O gaet ye me wi' naething ?
Rock and reel, and spinning wheel,
  A mickle quarter basin :
Bye attour, my gutcher has
  A heigh house and a laigh ane.
A' forbye my bonie sel,
  The toss o' Ecclefechan.

O haud your tongue now, Lucky Lang,
  O haud your tongue and jauner ;
I held the gate till you I met,
  Syne I began to wander :
I tint my whistle and my sang,
  I tint my peace and pleasure ;
But your green graff, now, Lucky Lang,
  Wad airt me to my treasure.

AY WAUKIN', O

Chorus

Ay waukin', O,
  Waukin' still and weary ;
Sleep I can get nane,
  For thinking on my dearie.

Summer's a pleasant time ;
  Flowers of ev'ry colour,
The water rins o'er the heugh,
  And I long for my true lover.

When I sleep I dream,
  When I wauk I'm eerie ;
Sleep I can get nane,
  For thinking on my dearie.

Lanely night comes on,
  A' the lave are sleepin' ;
I think on my dear lad,
  And bleer my een wi' greetin'.

TO DAUNTON ME

THE blude red rose at Yule may blaw,
The simmer lilies bloom in snaw,
The frost may freeze the deepest sea ;
But an auld man shall never daunton me.

Refrain
To daunton me, to daunton me,
An auld man shall never daunton me.

To daunton me, and me sae young,
Wi' his fause heart and flatt'ring tongue,
That is the thing you shall never see,
For an auld man shall never daunton me.
To daunton me, etc.

For a' his meal and a' his maut,
For a' his fresh beef and his saut,
For a' his gold and white monie,
An auld man shall never daunton me.
To daunton me, etc.

His gear may buy him kye and yowes,
His gear may buy him glens and knowes ;
But me he shall not buy nor fee,
For an auld man shall never daunton me.
To daunton me, etc.

He hirples twa-fauld as he dow,
Wi' his teethless gab and his auld beld pow,
And the rain rains down frae his red blear'd
    e'e ;
That auld man shall never daunton me.
        To daunton me, etc.

A ROSE-BUD BY MY EARLY WALK

A ROSE-BUD by my early walk,
Adown a corn-enclosèd bawk,
Sae gently bent its thorny stalk,
    All on a dewy morning.
Ere twice the shades o' dawn are fled,
In a' its crimson glory spread,
And drooping rich the dewy head,
    It scents the early morning.

Within the bush her covert nest
A little linnet fondly prest ;
The dew sat chilly on her breast,
    Sae early in the morning.
She soon shall see her tender brood,
The pride, the pleasure o' the wood,
Amang the fresh green leaves bedew'd,
    Awake the early morning.

So thou, dear bird, young Jeany fair,
On trembling string or vocal air,
Shall sweetly pay the tender care
    That tents thy early morning.
So thou, sweet Rose-bud, young and gay,
Shall beauteous blaze upon the day,
And bless the parent's evening ray
    That watch'd thy early morning.

THE POSIE

O LUVE will venture in where it daurna weel
    be seen,
O luve will venture in where wisdom ance hath
    been ;
But I will doun yon river rove, amang the
    wood sae green,
    And a' to pu' a Posie to my ain dear May.

The primrose I will pu', the firstling o' the year,
And I will pu' the pink, the emblem of my
    dear ;
For she's the pink o' womankind, and blooms
    without a peer,
    And a' to be a Posie to my ain dear May.

I'll pu' the budding rose, when Phœbus peeps
    in view,
For it's like a baumy kiss o' her sweet, bonnie
    mou' ;
The hyacinth's for constancy wi' its unchanging
    blue,
    And a' to be a Posie to my ain dear May.

The lily it is pure, and the lily it is fair,
And in her lovely bosom I'll place the lily
    there ;

The daisy's for simplicity and unaffected air,
   And a' to be a Posie to my ain dear May.

The hawthorn I will pu', wi' its locks o' siller
      gray,
Where, like an aged man, it stands at break o'
      day ;
But the songster's nest within the bush I winna
      tak away,
   And a' to be a Posie to my ain dear May.

The woodbine I will pu', when the e'ening star
      is near,
And the diamond draps o' dew shall be her een
      sae clear ;
The violet's for modesty, which weel she fa's
      to wear,
   And a' to be a Posie to my ain dear May.

I'll tie the Posie round wi' the silken band o'
      luve,
And I'll place it in her breast, and I'll swear
      by a' above,
That to my latest draught o' life the band shall
      ne'er remove,
   And this will be a Posie to my ain dear May.

SIC A WIFE AS WILLIE HAD

WILLIE WASTLE dwalt on Tweed,
  The spot they ca'd it Linkumdoddie.
Willie was a wabster gude,
  Could stown a clue wi' ony body :
He had a wife was dour and din,
  O Tinkler Maidgie was her mither ;
Sic a wife as Willie had,
  I wad na gie a button for her.

She had an e'e, she has but ane,
  The cat has twa the very colour ;
Five rusty teeth, forbye a stump,
  A clapper tongue wad deave a miller ;
A whiskin beard about her mou',
  Her nose and chin they threaten ither ;
Sic a wife as Willie had,
  I wad na gie a button for her.

She's bow-hough'd, she's hen-shin'd,
  Ae limpin' leg a hand-breed shorter ;
She's twisted right, she's twisted left,
  To balance fair in ilka quarter :
She has a hump upon her breast,
  The twin o' that upon her shouther ;
Sic a wife as Willie had,
  I wad na gie a button for her.

Auld baudrons by the ingle sits
    An' wi' her loof her face a-washin' ;
But Willie's wife is nae sae trig,
    She dights her grunzie wi' a hushion :
Her walie nieves like midden-creels,
    Her face wad fyle the Logan Water ;
Sic a wife as Willie had,
    I wad na gie a button for her.

SHE SAYS SHE LO'ES ME
BEST OF A'

Sae flaxen were her ringlets,
  Her eyebrows of a darker hue,
Bewitchingly o'er-arching
  Twa laughing een o' lovely blue ;
Her smiling, sae wyling,
  Wad make a wretch forget his woe ;
What pleasure, what treasure,
  Unto these rosy lips to grow !
Such was my Chloris' bonnie face,
  When first that bonnie face I saw
And ay my Chloris' dearest charm—
  She says she lo'es me best of a'.

Like harmony her motion,
  Her pretty ankle is a spy
Betraying fair proportion,
  Wad make a saint forget the sky :
Sae warming, sae charming,
  Her faultless form and gracefu' air ;
Ilk feature—auld Nature
  Declar'd that she could do nae mair :
Hers are the willing chains o' love,
  By conquering Beauty's sovereign law,
And still my Chloris' dearest charm—
  She says she lo'es me best of a'.

Let others love the city,
    And gaudy show, at sunny noon ;
Gie me the lonely valley,
    The dewy eve, and rising moon,
Fair beaming, and streaming,
    Her silver light the boughs amang ;
While falling, recalling,
    The amorous thrush concludes his sang :
Then, dearest Chloris, wilt thou rove,
    By wimpling burn and leafy shaw,
And hear my vows o' truth and love,
    And say thou lo'es me best of a'.

INDEX OF FIRST LINES

GLOSSARY

A', *all.*

Abeigh *or* Abiegh, *at a shy distance.*

Aboon *or* Abune, *above.*

Acquent, *acquainted.*

Ae, *one.*

Aiblins, *perhaps; may be.*

Aiken, *oaken.*

Ain, *own.*

Airle-penny, *fee-penny.*

Airt, *direction; to direct.*

Aith, *oath.*

Ajee, *to one side.*

Amang, *among.*

An', *and.*

Ance, *once.*

Ane, *one.*

Anither, *another.*

Asklent, *aslant; obliquely.*

Aucht *or* Aught, *eight; to own.*

Auld, *old.*

Auld lang syne, *long, long ago.*

Awa', *away.*

Awee, *a little.* Bide awee, *wait a minute.*

Ay, *yes; always.*

Ba', *ball; a ball.*

Baith, *both.*

Bannock, *a round flat cake.*

Barefit, *barefooted.*

Barley-bree *or* Barley-broo, *juice of barley; whisky.*

Baudrons, *a cat.*

Bauld, *bold.*

Baumy, *balmy.*

Bawk, *a ridge left untilled.*

Bear *or* Bere, *barley.*

Beet, *to fan; to feed; to warm.*

Befa', *befall.*

Beld, *bald.*

Ben, *in.* Ben-end, *inner end; the parlour.*

Bide, *to stay; abide.*

Biel' *or* Bield, *shelter; habitation.*

Big, *to build.*

Birk, *the birch.*

Birkie, *a plucky little fellow.*

Blaw, *to boast; to blow.*

Blear't *or* Blearit, *bedimmed with weeping.*

Blin', *blind.*

Blink, *a moment; a glance; a smile.*

Blinks, *look smilingly.*

Bluid *or* Blude, *blood.*

Blunty, *a stupid person.*

Bogle, *a hobgoblin.*

Bonie *or* Bonnie, *beautiful; sweet-looking.*

Bow-hough'd, *bandy-legged.*

Brae, *the slope of a small hill.*

Braid, *broad.*

Braw, *gallant; handsome; finely dressed.*

Breckan, *fern.*

Bree, *juice; liquid.*

Breeks, *breeches.*

Brent, *polished.*

Brulzie, *a broil; a quarrel.*

Bughtin-time, *the time for gathering the sheep into the fold for the night.*

Burn *or* Burnie, *a rivulet.*

But and ben, *kitchen and parlour.*

By attour, *aside and at a distance.*

Ca', *call; to drive.*

Ca'd or Ca't, *called; driven; also calved.*

Cam', *came.*

Canna, *cannot.*

Cannie, *gentle; mild.*

Cantie or Canty, *cheerful; lively.*

Cauld, *cold.*

Chitterin', *shivering with cold.*

Clamb, *did climb.*

Claught, *caught.*

Claut, *to scrape.* A claut, *a handful.*

Claver, *clover.*

Claw, *to scratch.*

Cleed, *to clothe.*

Clink, *a sharp stroke; money; rhyme.*

Clue, *a ball of yarn or twine.*

Coft, *bought.*

Cog, *a wooden dish.*

Coila or Kyle, *a district in Ayrshire.*

Coof or Cuif, *a blockhead; a ninny.*

Coost, *did cast.*

Couthie or couthy, *kind; loving.*

Crap, *a crop; did creep.*

Craw, *a crow; to crow.*

Crouse, *brisk and bold.*

Cushat, *wood-pigeon.*

Daur, *dare.* Daur't, *dared.*

Daw, *dawn.*

Dearie, *diminutive of dear; sweetheart.*

Deave, *to deafen.*

Deils, *devils.*

Dight, *to winnow corn; to wipe.*

Dochter, *daughter.*

Dool, *sorrow.*

Douce, *sober; prudent; wise.*

Dour, *obstinate.*

Dour and din, *stubborn and sallow.*

Dow, *can.* The best he dow, *the best he can.*

Dowff, *pithless.*

Doylt or Doylte, *stupefied; crazed.*

Dozen't, *benumbed.*

Draigl't, *draggled; dirty and wet.*

Drap, *a drop.*

Drappie, *diminutive of drap.*

Dreigh, *tedious; long about it.*

Drouket or Droukit, *soaked; drenched.*

Drumly, *muddy.*

Dunt, *blow.*

Dunted, *beaten.*

Dwalt, *dwelt.*

Ee or E'e, *eye.*

Een, *eyes.* E'en, *even.* E'en's, *even as.*

E'en or E'enin, *the evening.*

Eerie, *ghostly; fear-inspiring.*

Eild, *old age.*

Eller, *an elder of the church.*

Fa', *fall; lot; try.*

Fairly, *evenly; entirely.*

Faucht, *fought; a fight.*

Fauld, *a fold for sheep.*

Faulding, *folding.*

Fause, *false.*

Faut, *fault.*

Fecht, *to fight; a fight.*

Fell, *keen; biting; nippy.*

Fen or Fend, *to shift; successful effort.*

Fient, *fiend; a petty oath.*

Fiere, *comrade ; friend.*
Fit, *foot ; footstep.*
Flang, *threw with violence ; danced wildly.*
Flee, *a fly ; to fly.*
Fleech, *to supplicate ; to wheedle.*
Fley, *to frighten.*
Foor, *fared.*
Forby *or* Forbye, *besides.*
Fou *or* Fu' *full ; drunk.*
Frae, *from.*
Fu', *full.*
Fyle, *to soil ; to dirty.*

Gab, *the mouth.* To gab, *to speak fluently.*
Gaed, *went.*
Gaen *or* Gane, *gone.*
Gaet *or* Gate, *way ; manner.*
Gang, *to go ; to walk.*
Gar, *to compel ; to make.*
Gat, *got.*
Gate. *See* Gaet.
Gaud, *goad ; the ploughstaff.*
Gear, *wealth ; goods.*
Geck, *to toss the head in scorn.*
Ghaist, *ghost.*
Gie, *to give.* Gies, *gives.* Gied, *gave.* Gien, *given.*
Gie's, *give us.*
Gif, *if.*
Gin, *if ; by.*
Gloamin', *gloaming ; twilight.*
Glow'r, *to stare ; a stare in wonder.*
Gotten, *got.*
Gowan, *the wild or mountain daisy.*
Gowd, *gold.*
Graff, *the grave.*
Graith, *harness.*
Grat, *wept.*

Gree, *to agree ; superiority.* To bear the gree, *to win the victory.*
Grunzie, *the mouth or snout.*
Gude *or* Guid, *good ; the Supreme Being.*
Gude-willie, *with good will.*
Gude-willie waucht, *a drink with right good will.*
Gutcher, *grandfather.*

Ha', *hall.*
Hae, *have ; to accept.* Haen, *had.* Hae't, *have it.*
Haet, *the least thing.* Fient-haet, *nothing at all.*
Hairst, *harvest.*
Haith, *a petty oath.*
Hale, *whole ; healthy ; well.*
Hallowe'en, *Hallowmas Eve.*
Haly, *holy.*
Hame, *home.* Hamely, *homely ; familiar.*
Han', *hand.*
Han'-breed, *a hand-breadth.*
Hansel, *a first gift.*
Haud, *hold.*
Hauf, *half.*
Hecht, *promised.*
Heich *or* Heigh, *high.*
Heugh, *a hollow.*
Heuk, *a hook.*
Hie, *high.*
Hiney, *honey.* Hinny, *sweet.*
Hing, *to hang.*
Hirple, *to walk haltingly.*
Hirplin', *limping.*
Hizzie, *a lively young woman.*
Hoast, *a cough.*
Hodden-grey, *coarse grey woollen cloth.*
Hoddin', *hobbling.*
Hushion, *a footless stocking.*

Ilk or Ilka, *each ; every.*
Ingle-lowe, *the flame of the fire.*
Ither, *other.*

Jad or Jaud, *a jade.*
Janwar, *January.*
Jauner, *idle talk.*
Jo, *a sweetheart, joy.*

Keek, *a sly look ; to peep.*
Keekit, *peeped.*
Ken, *to know.*
Kent, *knew.*
Kin', *kind.*
Knowe, *a hillock.*
Knurl, *a churl.*
Kye, *kine ; cows.*

Laddie, *diminutive of* lad.
Laigh, *low.*
Lan', *land.*
Lane, *lone.*
Lang, *long.*
Lang syne, *long ago.*
Lassie, *diminutive of* lass.
Lave, *the rest. The lave, the others.*
Lav'rock, *the lark.*
Lea-rig, *grass ridge.*
Leal, *loyal ; true.*
Lear, *learning ; lore.*
Lee-lang, *live-long.*
Leesome, *pleasant.*
Leeze me, *a phrase of endearment.*
Leugh, *did laugh.*
Leuk, *look, appearance.*
Libbet, *castrated.*
Liein, *telling lies.*
Linn, *a waterfall ; a cascade.*
Lint-white, *flaxen-coloured.*
Lo'ed, *loved.* Lo'esome, *lovesome.*

Loof, *the palm of the hand.*
Loot, *let.*
Loun, *a low fellow.*
Loup or Lowp, *leap.*
Lour, *frown, sullen, dark threatening.*

Mahoun, *Satan.*
Mailen or Mailin, *a farm.*
Mailie, *Molly.*
Mair, *more.*
Mak', *make ; shape.*
Mark, *merk (an ancient Scottish coin), value thirteen shillings and fourpence.*
Maun, *must.* Mauna, *must not.*
Maut, *malt.*
Mavis, *thrush.*
Mawn, *mown ; a basket.*
Meikle, Mickle, or Muckle, *big ; much.*
Midden-creels, *dung-baskets.*
Minnie, *mother.*
Mirk, *dark.*
Mither, *mother.*
Monie or Mony, *many.*
Mou', *mouth.*
Mysel', *myself.*

Na or Nae, *no.*
Naebody, *nobody.*
Naig, *a horse ; a nag.*
Nane, *none.*
Neebors, *neighbours.*
Neist or Niest, *next.*
Niest, *next.*
Nieve or Nief, *the fist.*
Nocht, *nothing.*

O', *of.*
O ! Oh ! Och ! Ochone ! *exclamations of distress or longing.*

154

O'erword, *refrain; a phrase often repeated.*
Onie or Ony, *any.*
O't, *of it.*
Ower or Owre, *over.*
Owsen, *oxen.*

Paidle, *to paddle.*
Paidl'd, *paddled.*
Pint-stoup, *a two-quart measure.*
Plaiden, *coarse woollen cloth.*
Plew or Pleugh, *plough.*
Poortith, *poverty.*
Pouch, *pocket.*
Pou'd, Pou't, or Pu'd, *pulled.*
Pow, *the head; the poll.*
Pree or Prie, *to taste.*
Pu', *to pull.*

Quean, *a young woman; a lass.*

Rant, *an unskilled song; to rollick.*
Rantin, *joyous; free.*
Rig, *a ridge.*
Rin, *run.*
Roose, *to praise; to flatter.*
Roun', *round.*
Rowes, *rolls.*
Rowthie, *having plenty.*

Sae, *so.*
Saft, *soft.*
Sair, *sore; to serve.*
Sairly, *sorely.*
Sang, *song; did sing.*
Sark, *a shirt.*
Saut, *salt.*
Sel', *self.*
Shachl'd, *shapeless.*
Shaw, *show; a wooded dell.*

Shiel or Shielin', *a hut; a shepherd's cottage; a shelter.*
Shill, *shrill.*
Shoon, *shoes.*
Shouther, *shoulder.*
Shure, *did shear (corn).*
Sic, *such.* Siccan, *such-like.*
Siller, *silver; money in general.*
Simmer, *summer.*
Sinny, *sunny.*
Skeigh, *high-mettled; proud.*
Skelp, *a slap; to run.*
Sliddery, *slippery.*
Sma', *small.*
Smoor'd, *smothered.*
Snapper, *to stumble in walking.*
Snaw, *snow.*
Snool, *to cringe; sneak.*
Sodger or Soger, *a soldier.*
Sowther, *to solder; to make up.*
Spak, *spake.*
Speer or Spier, *to inquire; to ask.*
Stack, *stuck; a rick of hay or corn.*
Staw, *a stall; stole; to surfeit.*
Sten', *to leap; to rear, as a horse.*
Stockit, *stocked.*
Stound, *a sudden pang of the heart.*
Stoup or Stowp, *a measure with a handle for serving liquids.*
Stoure, *dust in motion; excitement.*
Stowlins, *by stealth.*
Stown, *stolen.*
Stoyte, *to stagger.*
Strappin, *tall and handsome.*
Swoor, *swore.*
Syne, *then; since.*

Ta'en, *taken*.
Tapsalteerie, *topsy-turvy*.
Tassie, *a drinking-cup; a goblet, generally of silver*.
Tauld or **Tald**, *told*.
Temper-pin, *the regulating pin of a spinning-wheel*.
Tent, *to take heed; mark*.
Thegither, *together*.
Till't, *to it*. Fa' till't, *begin*.
Timmer, *timber; a tree*.
Tine or **Tyne**, *to lose*.
Tint, *lost*.
Tinkler, *a tinker*.
Tocher, *dowry; marriage portion*.
Towmond, *a twelvemonth*.
Trow, *to believe*.
Trowth, *troth; a petty oath*.
Twa, *two*.

Unco, *strange; uncouth; very*.
Unfauld, *unfold*.

Vittle, or **Victual**, *grain*.

Wa', *wall*.
Wab, *web*.
Wabster, *weaver*.
Wad, *would; wager; wed*.
Wadna, *would not*.
Wae, *woe; sad*.
Waefu', *woeful*.
Wale, *choice; to choose*.
Walie, *ample; jolly; large*.
Walie ! *an exclamation of distress*.

Wark, *work*.
Warlock, *a wizard*.
Warl'y, *worldly*.
Warsle or **Warstle**, *to wrestle*.
Warst, *worst*.
Wat, *wet*. I wat, *I know*.
Waught, *a copious drink*.
Wauken, *awake; to awaken*.
Waukening, *awakening*.
Waukin', *waking*.
Waur, *worse; to worst*.
Wee, *little*.
Weel, *well*. Weelfare, *welfare*.
Weet, *wet; to wet; rain*.
Wha, *who*.
Whar or **Whare**, *where*.
Whase, *whose*.
Wha's, *whose; who is*.
Whittle, *a clasp-knife*.
Whyles, *sometimes*.
Wi', *with*.
Widdiefu', *gallows-worthy*.
Wight, *strong*.
Wimplin', *meandering*.
Win', *wind; the wind*.
Winna, *will not*.
Winsome, *attractive*.
Wyle, *to decoy; to entice*.

Yestreen, *yesternight*.
Yett, *gate*.
Yill, *ale*.
Yon, *yonder*. Yon time, *yonder time*.
Yowe, *a ewe*.
Yowes, *ewes*.

CHRONOLOGICAL LIST OF THE
SONGS IN THIS EDITION
(*so far as known*)

1775

O Tibbie, I hae seen the day.

1780

The Lass of Cessnock Banks.
Mary Morison.

1782

John Barleycorn

1783

The Rigs o' Barley—" It was upon a Lammas
    night."
Now Westlin Winds.
My Nannie O—" Behind yon hills."

1784

Green grow the Rashes, O.

1785

Rantin', Rovin' Robin.
Young Peggy.

1786

Farewell to St. James's Lodge.
The Lass o' Ballochmyle.
The gloomy night.
On Sensibility.

1787

Here's a bottle.
Birks of Aberfeldy.
A Rose-bud by my Early Walk.
Banks of Devon.

1788

Clarinda, Mistress of my Soul.
Owre Young to Marry yet.
Up in the morning.
Duncan Davidson.
The Blude-red Rose.
O a' the Airts.
I hae a wife o' my ain.
Anna, thy charms.
Go, fetch to me a Pint o' Wine.
Auld Lang Syne.
Robin shure in Hairst.
On a Bank of Flowers.
Young Jockey.
John Anderson, my jo.
My Love, she's but a Lassie yet.
Tam Glen.
Whistle o'er the Lave o't.
Willie brew'd a Peck o' Maut.
Ca' the Yowes.
Farewell to the Highlands.
To Mary in Heaven

1791

Out over the Forth.
Ye banks and braes o' bonnie Doon.
Craigieburn Wood.
The Bonnie Wee Thing.

What can a Young Lassie do.
The Posie.
The Gallant Weaver.
My Tocher's the Jewel.
O for Ane an' Twenty, Tam !
Fair Eliza—" Turn again."
Sweet Afton.
Sensibility.
Ae Fond Kiss.

1792

Willie Wastle.
The De'il's awa wi' the Exciseman.
Country Lassie—" In simmer when the hay."
The Lea Rig—" When o'er the hill."
My Wife's a Winsome Wee Thing.
Highland Mary—" Ye banks and braes."
Duncan Gray.

1793

Poortith Cauld—" O why should Fate."
Braw, braw Lads.
Wandering Willie.
Meg o' the Mill.
The Soldier's Return.
O were my Love yon Lilac Fair.
Bonnie Jean.
Whistle, and I'll come to you, my Lad.
Dainty Davie.
Scots wha hae.

1794

Wilt thou be my Dearie ?
Bannocks o' bear meal.